Praise for *Out of the Ashes*

The Phoenix is a bird that rises out of its ashes to a new life. The congregation Ken serves is Phoenix Community Church, United Church of Christ, a gathering of people who too often have suffered in other churches and now claim a new life together. Ken grew up in a more fundamentalist congregation to find the freedom offered by a new and more liberating expression of the Christian faith, from the hierarchy of kingdom to the collegiality of kin-dom. Ken's background in computer science shows through in the thoroughness of his exploration and exhortation. His journey led him to Master's degrees in computer science and in theology prior to earning his M.Div. His life has truly been a pilgrimage, a search for meaning and purpose that includes belief and behavior as well as belonging. As he describes his text, it is "for those burned out on traditional Christianity." Each chapter concludes with discussion questions that invite the reader to join in the search and make the book a perfect resource for group conversation. We are all in search of a genuine faith and we have all been burned at some time. There is a phoenix in each of us, waiting to arise!

Dr. David Moffett-Moore
Pastor, Portage United Church of Christ
Author of Creation in Contemporary Experrience

In *Out of the Ashes*, Kenneth Arthur challenges his Christian readers to be open to questions about the Christian faith and how that faith has traditionally conceptualized God as "the given God" and the "Santa-for-adults God" and invites us to imagine love as the Divine Presence that pulls us to wholeness and one-ness with the Divine. Arthur does not ground his understanding of the Divine Presence in speculative theology, however; but in the incarnation of Jesus, which continues in the incarnation of the body of Christ. Moreover, Arthur is not simply dealing in theoretical concepts; he successfully intersperses his theological argument with real ministry experiences, particularly in the way the church he serves as pastor has implemented these ideas. The book is theologically rich, ministerially practical, and is a unique contribution to the continuing discussion regarding progressive Christianity. Individuals and groups interested in the progressive Christian movement should read this book.

C. Drew Smith
Author of *Reframing a Relevant Faith*

Bishop John Spong opened the door that invites people alienated from the church to take a fresh look at how Christianity can, again, become a vital part of human experience. Ken Arthur has walked through that door—even blown it wide open—and provides a reinvigorating restatement of the Christian experience that is both compelling and winsome. He offers fresh insights for now tired and unfulfilling notions of faith, not by redefining them, but reframing the biblical story in such a way that new understandings freely emerge. But it's not only for seekers: If you are presently on this path, your spirit will be strengthened and your horizons of the possible widened.

Rev. Steven Kindle
Author of *If Your Child is Gay, I'm Right and You're Wrong: Why We Disagree about the Bible and What to Do about It*

Out of the Ashes

Constructive Theology for Those Burned Out on Christianity

Kenneth W. Arthur

Energion Publications
Gonzalez, Florida
2017

Author photo credit: Dave Dietz

ISBN10: 1-63199-398-4
ISBN13: 978-1-63199-398-5
Library of Congress Control Number: 2017943423

Energion Publications
P. O. Box 841
Gonzalez, FL 32560

energion.com
pubs@energion.com

Dedication

This book is dedicated to the innumerable people who have nurtured my spiritual journey. I would like to especially mention my mother, Prudence L. Arthur; my childhood pastor, the late Rev. Harold L. Nelson; my pastoral mentors, the Rev. Janice Springer and the Rev. Whitney Brown; the professors of Chicago Theological Seminary; and the wonderful folks of Phoenix Community Church, United Church of Christ. Love to you all.

Table of Contents

Preface....................vii

1 An Elephant in the Dark....................1
Chapter 1 Discussion Questions 20
2 Naughty or Nice....................21
Chapter 2 Discussion Questions 31
3 The Electrifying Gravity of Love....................33
Burns, Morisette, or Freeman: Old Metaphors 33
The Power You're Supplying, It's Electrifying:
New Metaphors 37
Messy Incarnation: Unity and Multiplicity 42
Divine Mathematics: The Trinity 48
Chapter 3 Discussion Questions 51
4 In Our Image....................53
We've Fallen and Can't Get Up:
The Human Situation 53
The Deathly Hallows: Incarnations of Divinity 59
Woven Together in Love: Community 64
Chapter 4 Discussion Questions 78
5 Separated but Together....................79
Neither Naughty nor Nice: Defining Sin 79
The Devil is in the Details: Manifestations of Sin 84
Threat of Apocalypse:
Searching for a Christian Response to War 88
Why Have You Forsaken Me: Suffering and Evil 99
Chapter 5 Discussion Questions 103
6 A Light for the World....................105
One Night in Bethlehem: Jesus as Incarnation 105
Loving the World: Jesus' Life and Ministry 107
The Queer Christ: Jesus as Multiplicity 109
On the Cross: Salvation 112
Returning to the Divine: Seeking Forgiveness 117

Chapter 6 Discussion Questions 124
7 Realizing the Kin-dom 125
Ultimate Mystery: The Kin-dom in Heaven 125
Elusive Justice: The Kin-dom on Earth 132
Chapter 7 Discussion Questions 139
8 Loving Our Neighbor 141
Doing the work of the Divine:
Co-creating the Kin-dom 141
Responding to the Divine: Church and Worship 144
Called by the Divine: Ministry 156
Chapter 8 Discussion Questions 159

Bibliography 161

Preface

This work represents my deepest yearning for my ministry, that all people may come to know the Presence of the Divine in their life despite the failings of the Christian church and Christ's all too human followers. Frequently, what we understand the church or Christianity to be ceases to have significance in our lives. We see church oppression and hypocrisy and, not knowing any alternative, we try to put Mystery behind us, neglecting our spiritual dimension and even declaring God to be dead.

My hope is that we will not let the failings of the church keep us from seeking deeper meaning in our journey through this life, whether it be Christianity or some other path of spiritual discovery. For those interested or grounded in Christianity, know that there is not just one Christian perspective. In writing this book, I hope to help readers open themselves to some of the alternatives to the fundamentalist and often oppressive Christianity that is too often assumed to represent all followers of Christ. We don't need to just accept what a sensationalist media or our traditional patriarchal institutions dictate to us. There is room for new learning and new understandings. We don't need to reject everything that has been handed down to us either. In the end we may find much wisdom in what we've been taught or rediscover important teachings that have been tossed to the sidelines of our faith.

I am not trying to provide definitive answers to any of the questions we might have about our faith. However, instead of throwing the baby Jesus out with the bathwater as we can be tempted to do, I hope readers will be inspired to seek their own understandings and their own relationship with Divine Mystery. To that end, I have also included a few questions at the end of each chapter that I hope will be useful for both individual reflection and group discussions.

This book represents a large part of my own spiritual journey and much of it derives from work I did while in seminary and from sermons I've written as a parish pastor. The basis of this book is a constructive theology paper that was the capstone of my Master of Divinity degree at Chicago Theological Seminary. The theology that I propose herein keeps a constructive focus. That is, the view of the Divine presented considers and builds upon many different sources including scripture and the work of other theologians.

I also want to acknowledge the important role the people of Phoenix Community Church, United Church of Christ, in Kalamazoo, Michigan, have had in my journey. My experiences with this wonderful community of seekers has had a correspondingly significant influence on the reflections contained within this book and that church's theological underpinnings are one of the sources I ask us to reflect upon. I would also like to thank the Rev. David Moffett-Moore, the Rev. Janice Springer, and the Phoenix Community Church book study group, for reviewing drafts of this work and providing invaluable feedback and encouragement.

May the Presence of the Divine bless you, the reader, on your own journey to find wholeness.

Kenneth W. Arthur
November 6, 2016

1 An Elephant in the Dark

The Project Ahead

Have you come to doubt your Christian beliefs? Perhaps what you know as Christian teachings hasn't matched your own life experiences. Perhaps the answers that Christians have given to life's deep mysteries don't ring true for you. Perhaps you have been disenfranchised by the many people who make outlandish claims or hateful condemnations in the name of Christianity. Perhaps what you hear passed off as Christianity contradicts scientific understanding as well as common sense. Indeed, much of what passes for Christianity in today's world, and especially the media, is truly disturbing. Who would want to follow a God whose ordained representatives call for the death of abortion doctors or gay people, for example?

Unfortunately, many Christians adhere to doctrines and beliefs that are stuck in out-dated understandings of God and the world. Fundamentalism is a disturbing religious manifestation in every religion - not just Christianity - and refuses to be questioned, instead clinging to its own answers no matter how ridiculous they seem. However, despite what one might conclude from how Christianity is represented in the media, fundamentalists do not speak for all of Christianity. There are millions of thinking Christians who manage to maintain a deep faith that encourages questions without dictating simplistic answers, seeks to understand God in the context of our scientific understanding rather than in opposition to it, and that embraces all people as worthy of God's love. In other words, a reasonable rejection of fundamentalism does not mean we have to reject Christianity or God.

Among those of us who have been alienated by religion and Christianity in particular, many still have some kind of belief in God or a higher power even if we struggle to explain it. We ask ourselves: Who or what is God? Does God even exist? To ask these questions is to be human. Pondering the existence of a being or power which is greater than ourselves is a fundamental human experience. Everyone has at least thought about these questions even if the answers we arrive at individually are wildly different. Some people understand God to be a father, a wise old man, or a judge. Some people understand God to actually be Goddess, a feminine figure and perhaps a mother. Some people might think of God as an energy of some kind. There are many ways that human beings understand God. Some people, of course, would say that God does not exist. Even then, such people usually have a specific image of God which they argue against.

In the end, no matter how we envision God we cannot conclusively prove either that God exists or doesn't exist, at least not within the bounds of current human knowledge. For those who see lack of scientific proof as evidence of the non-existence of God, I will not be able to convince them otherwise and don't intend to try. I can't prove that love exists either, but I believe it does because I have experienced it. Likewise, my own personal experience leads me to believe that there is a greater power in this universe, a mystery which I call God.

For me, the critical question is not whether God exists. Instead, the critical question is: who or what is God and what is our relationship to this higher power? What we believe or don't believe about God affects our lives greatly. I've heard it said that what we do as Christians, or as followers of God, is much more important than what we believe. I think this is true. Treating each other with love, compassion, and respect is much more important than what we believe happens during the sacrament of communion, for example.

However, our theology, what we believe about God and each other is still important. Our beliefs deeply impact the formation of our culture and our individual behavior, affecting everyone around us, including those who remain unconvinced of God's existence. Our beliefs about God inform and are informed by our morals, our ideals, our principles, what we think is acceptable and what is not.

From an early age, we are all instilled with certain concepts and notions of who or what God is or is not. As a child growing up in a Protestant Christian tradition, I was given concepts of God through the teachings of my family, church, and culture. These were given to me both in the sense of *handed over to* and also in the sense that they were often simply accepted by me and assumed as truths, or *givens*. As I got older, I found that the so-called truths of these given concepts no longer corresponded with my personal experience of God.

Questioning what we are taught as children is a normal and critical part of growing up and becoming mature, self-differentiated human beings. As children, we tend to accept what we are told as the truth. Growing older and more independent, we learn by asking "why?" And when what we've been taught doesn't fit a certain situation, we are confronted with a crisis of discontinuity. When it comes to God, realizing a discontinuity between what we are taught and what we experience in life is not at all uncommon. We have three choices when that happens: we can take the fundamentalist approach and deny the reality of our experience, clinging to our beliefs and striking out at anything that might question them; we can abandon our faith altogether; or we can ask questions and struggle with our faith as we search for new understandings.

Experiencing discontinuity in one's beliefs about God is particularly common for queer people such as myself.[1] It has been my

1 The term "queer" can still be controversial. Although the word may have derogatory connotations for many people, it has been largely reclaimed, especially among younger people and in the academic world. As an adjective or noun, I mean to use it as a catch-all word referring to lesbian, gay, bisexual, and transgender people as well as any others who don't fit into our culture's norm of heterosexuality or the standard male/female dichotomy. Therefore, as a gay man, I also identify myself as queer. As a verb, queer may be understood as implying the transgression of our culture's norms surrounding sexuality and gender. For example, supporting same-sex marriage is "to queer" the institution of marriage because such support transgresses and challenges the expectation of marriage as being between a man and a woman, which is based both on the norm of heterosexuality and the male/female dichotomy.

observation that queer people often come to a point in their lives where they encounter discontinuities between their lived experiences and their images and understandings of God. For example, a lesbian may experience her love for another woman as natural and proper, but be told through the teachings of many churches that her love, and therefore her very being and essence as a human, is unacceptable to God. When this happens, her life experience and her concept of God no longer correspond.

Of course, such experiences of discontinuity are not solely the province of queer people. There are many reasons we may come to experience such a discontinuity, depending on what we have been taught about God. For example, one might, as I did as a teenager, have problems reconciling the images of a forgiving, loving God who welcomes everyone with a judging God who punishes bad people for eternity in hell. For others, a tragedy may lead them to question the image of an all-controlling, loving God who seems unwilling to act to prevent senseless suffering.

Experiences of discontinuity in our beliefs, when we are unable to reconcile our images of God with our life experiences, may lead some people to conclude that God does not exist. Perhaps even more disturbing, some people may cling to their given images of God and conclude that they themselves are somehow defective. However, others find their way to new, liberated, and for them, more meaningful concepts of God.

In the following pages, I will attempt to undertake an exploration of the Divine that reflects my own search. I will try to discover a new, more meaningful understanding of God by using as a starting point a *given God* concept which has proven lacking. Certainly, I don't think that everything I was taught as a child about God was wrong. Indeed, I still treasure many of the lessons of my childhood. However, some of what I am calling my given concepts of God have failed to measure up to my life experiences. Because of this they provide a foundation for a sense of what God is not. Considering what God is not, we can then consider what

God might be. We are able to look for an unknown God waiting to be discovered but currently hidden by the given God.

The God-talk I will use and the propositions I might make about God and human spirituality are from a Christian perspective and use Christian language because Christianity is both my given and chosen path. This is not to say that Christianity is in any way superior to any other religious path. Indeed, all religions can learn much from each other. However, to talk deeply about religious and spiritual questions, it seems helpful and perhaps even necessary to use a single framework of language and concepts.

As I've heard it stated before, we might think of God as the center of a wheel with each spoke representing a different religion. To really approach closely to God we need to choose a spoke and travel down its path, rather than move from spoke to spoke along the surface of the wheel. The issue I would like to explore is what to do when the spoke we are traveling, Christianity, seems to no longer be getting us closer to God, when it seems as if it may be broken. What do we do when our given God, the traditional Christian concepts and images which we were taught, don't seem to be working for us anymore?

If our given God no longer holds truth for us, then we need to seek liberation from that god. The idea of a given God resonates with theologian James Evans' concept of the *ungiven* quality of God in African American liberation theology.[1] Evans names hiddenness as one of God's ungiven characteristics, pointing out how oppressed and marginalized people often experience God as hidden. When people are forced to live their lives hidden from the view of so-called proper society and when those lives so often lack clear meaning, God too becomes understood as embodying the same qualities of hiddenness and otherness. According to Evans, the ungiven character of God is also due to the inability of anyone to fully know God despite our experiences. Regardless of how forcefully God shows up in our lives, we can never fully know who or what God is or is not.

1 James H. Evans, Jr., *We Have Been Believers: An African American Systematic Theology*, 2nd ed. (Minneapolis: Fortress Press, 2012), 61-88.

When our old, tired, given God fails us, it is the search for the ungiven God, the as yet hidden and unknowable God, which holds the possibility of liberating us. Beginning from our failing given God, we will attempt to boldly seek out the ungiven God who can liberate us from ourselves. I do not expect, or even desire, that everyone will agree with my proposals. We must all come to our own conclusions about God. By providing alternative ways of thinking about God, my hope is that the reader will be inspired to a deeper faith through questioning and seeking their own answers.

It is not at all necessary to reject God because the given God has failed us. In the search for the ungiven God we can find hope within a loving Divine mystery. We can find the ungiven God patiently waiting for us, even lovingly reaching out to us as we reach out to the ungiven God.

If you choose to continue this journey with me, we will attempt to discover this ungiven God by utilizing important and appropriate sources of revelation — experience, theology, scripture, human culture and wisdom, and creation (or what we might also call nature) — as we consider the classical Christian theological subjects of God, humanity, sin and suffering, Christ, eschatology (end times), and ministry. Before we briefly consider each of the above revelatory sources, however, it is worthwhile to ask what revelation is.

A source of revelation reveals something of God to us because God is present in some way in that source. The well known theologian Paul Tillich called revelation a "special and extraordinary manifestation [of God] which removes the veil from something which is hidden."[1] However, revelation is not something that has happened once or twice and then never happens again. Any event or thing, ancient or new, can reveal the Divine and help us learn more about God. Tillich argued that nothing can be excluded from the possibility of revelation.[2] Revelation continues to happen ev-

1 Paul Tillich, *Systematic Theology, Vol. 1*, (Chicago: The University of Chicago Press, 1973), 108.

2 Ibid., 118.

erywhere and in every time because God is manifest everywhere and in every time.

This does not mean, however, that everything is necessarily a revelation of God. Along our journey, we must make some judgments about what reveals truth about God and what does not. One litmus test I would propose is whether the revelation is rooted in love. This may not always be clear, but it gives us a starting point. Jesus, upon whose life and teachings Christianity is based, stated that "all the law and the prophets" derive from the commandments to love God "with all your heart, and with all your soul, and with all your mind" and to love "your neighbor as yourself."[1] If in fact "all the law and the prophets," or all that we know about God, is based in love, then it seems to make good sense that a revelation of God would also be based in love in some way. At the very least, it should never lead us away from the commandment to love.

Let us now consider the mediums of revelation which will aid us on our journey in search of the ungiven God.

Experience. For James Evans, finding the ungiven God, the hidden and unknown God, begins in our own experiences and in the collective memory of our encounters with God.[2] When our individual experiences are joined together, they can become a powerful revelation. However, we must be careful that we are considering the collective witness of experience and not someone's individual experience, including our own, put forth falsely as the experience of all.

To guard against this, and since our individual experiences of the Holy join together to form our collective experience, I would propose that all sources of revelation must be considered in the light of one's personal experience of the Divine. We should never automatically assume that someone else's experience trumps our own. When considering an assertion about the Divine, we must always ask ourselves if that assertion resonates with our own experience of the Divine. If it doesn't then we may choose to set it aside for

1 Matthew 22:37-40

2 Evans, 61.

the time being, to be considered again later, or we may set it aside entirely, as we will some of the assertions about our given God.

For example, much of what I will propose about God is ultimately based on my own experiences. I will try to incorporate other sources for support and to form a collective experience of revelation. It is ultimately up to you to determine whether the theology within coincides with your own experiences of the Divine and whether this theology is meaningful to your life journey or not.

All sources of revelation are, in fact, filtered through experience. Tillich asserts that there are two components to revelation: the manifestation of God, or the "giving side," and the human experience of that manifestation, the "receiving side."[1] It is the act of receiving revelation that makes all revelation a subcategory of human experience and subject to human interpretation and human foibles. Because of this important fact, no source of revelation, all of which amount to human interpretations of human experience, can be granted an inherent preference over another. For example, while the Bible, which we will discuss in more depth shortly, is an important source of revelation for Christians, we cannot automatically assume it takes precedence over or has more authority than other sources of revelation. All sources of revelation are filtered through imperfect human interpretation.

Although all revelation must be considered in light of personal experience, seeking the ungiven God does not mean relying solely upon our personal experience, either. It must also be tempered and informed by the experiences of others. However important our personal experience is, to rely only on our own experiences and interpretations of them would produce a vastly incomplete and erroneous picture.

A poem attributed to the 13th century mystic Rumi describes several people led into a dark room where they find an unknown animal. Re-emerging from the room they variously describe a "water-pipe kind of creature," a "fan-animal," a "leathery throne," or a

1 Tillich, *Systematic Theology, Vol. 1*, 111.

"rounded sword of porcelain," all depending on which part of the mysterious animal they encounter. The poem concludes:

> Each of us touches one place
> and understands the whole in that way.
>
> The palm and the fingers feeling in the dark are
> how the senses explore the reality of the elephant.
>
> If each of us held a candle there,
> and if we went in together,
> we could see it.[1]

We must also remember that our experiences are moments in time. In the poem, if we first experienced the elephant as a fan-animal, the next time we encountered it we might touch a different part and find a leathery throne. Our experiences are not always the same. New experiences may reveal new truths about God. This is why collective experiences are important. Someone else's experience of God may reveal something we have not yet encountered.

If we are to attempt to know the hidden and unknowable God, then we must take seriously a wide range of experience. God has not only been present in history and in the lives of our faith ancestors, but continues to be present and manifest in all of our lives and in all of creation. As a result, the encounters of those ancestors with the Divine as passed down through the Bible, Christian tradition, and other writings need to be considered along with our personal experiences and the experiences of our contemporaries.

Theology. Simply put, theology is the study of God. According to James Evans, theology must be "experiential, metaphorical, analogical, and functional."[2] In other words, if theological discourse, or talk about the nature of God, is to be applicable to the

---

1 Maulana Jalal al-Din Rumi, *The Essential Rumi*, trans. Coleman Barks (San Francisco: HarperCollins Publishers, 1995), 252.

2 Evans, 62.

lives of those who are not academics, then it must be spoken in the language of the common person. Other theologians remind us that this God-talk should also not be mistaken for God. Sallie McFague states that no matter how well thought out our concepts of God, they are precisely *our* theology, *our* talk about God, and not actually God.[1] Likewise, Catherine Keller tantalizingly stresses that theology signifies "possibilities, not actualities."[2] We can never specify the nature of God definitively. We can never put God in a well-formed box and claim God is this or that and nothing more. Instead, our God-talk is about the possibilities of what God is or is not.

Paul Tillich makes this same point by noting that everything that can be said about God is symbolic.[3] God is ultimately unknowable in God's entirety. Because of this, metaphor becomes an important tool in theological discourse. McFague defines metaphor as trying to talk about the unfamiliar in terms of the familiar.[4] We use what we do know to think about things that we do not quite understand, as an approximation of what we don't know. Metaphors are never precise, but they are one of the best ways we have to reflect on the mysteries of life. In the course of our search for the ungiven God, I hope to say something about God through metaphor and analogy which invites us into the mystery, the story, of God, and encourages us to think and interpret for ourselves how that story might apply to our own lives. Like poetry, metaphor and analogy allow us to say something that cannot quite be said. They allow us to know something that cannot quite be known.

Theological reflections, in the form of the writings of theologians as well as church doctrines and dogmas, are important sources of revelation for our own theological musings. As a way of trying to formally understand who and what God is, theology is also a "disciplined and relational reflection upon" the faith and beliefs of past

1 Sallie McFague, *Models of God: Theology for an Ecological, Nuclear Age*, (Philadelphia: Fortress Press, 1987), 37.

2 Catherine Keller, *On the Mystery: Discerning Divinity in Process*, (Minneapolis: Fortress Press, 2008), 10.

3 Tillich, *Systematic Theology, Vol. 1*, 239.

4 McFague, *Models of God*, 33.

and present Christians.[1] Theology is relational because it reflects upon the relationship between God and Creation,[2] including us as human beings, and because those doing the reflecting necessarily participate in the relationship they are attempting to understand.[3]

Recognizing the relational-ness of our journey, it is important to acknowledge the importance of considering diverse experiences and hearing diverse theological voices. We will attempt to enter into relationship and be in conversation with several theologians of different backgrounds and perspectives. The most prominent, some of whom have already been mentioned above, are Patrick Cheng, Catherine Keller, Sallie McFague, and Paul Tillich. Patrick Cheng is a male, queer, Asian-American theologian, while Paul Tillich, originally from Germany, is a well known, white male voice among 20th century mainline, liberal theologians. Providing female voices are Sallie McFague, an ecological and metaphorical theologian, and Catherine Keller, a process theologian.[4] Both McFague and Keller also write from a feminist perspective. These theological voices as well as others will help inform our search for the ungiven God and contribute important insights from diverse viewpoints.

Scripture. Paul Tillich notes that the Bible is a basic source for theology because it is the document upon which the Christian church as we know it was founded. It contains the witness of some of the earliest followers of Christ, telling us how they understood the revelation of God in the events of their lives.[5] However, each of us has to decide how much authority we'll give the Bible and other religious texts in our own lives. While I understand the Bible as central to the Christian faith, it is a foundation to be built upon and not necessarily the last word on all issues.

---

1 Keller, *On the Mystery*, 17.

2 McFague, *Models of God*, 32.

3 Tillich, *Systematic Theology, Vol. 1*, 44.

4 Put simplistically, process theology uses a relational worldview in which God doesn't control us but is in relationship with us. For more detailed discussion see http://processandfaith.org/ or http://www.ctr4process.org/.

5 Ibid., 35.

Because it provides a common base for what we as Christians believe, we must take the Bible seriously whether we like what it says or not. There is much about the Bible on which Christians do not agree. We don't all need to understand and interpret it in the same way, but if we are to search for God within the framework of Christianity, then we each need to arrive at an understanding of how we will approach the Bible. I believe the Bible contains wisdom inspired by humanity's search for God, love of God, and desire to make sense of an oftentimes senseless world. The Bible reveals God but it does so through human knowledge, human experience, human interpretation, and human expression. It can show us a path to God, but that doesn't mean we have to agree or follow all that is written in its pages. Those words, as a product of human experience, also need to be subject to the litmus test of love.

It is good and necessary to recognize that the Bible is not always easy to read and understand. Tillich notes that biblical writings, although they are a witness of revelation, are conditioned by and expressions of the authors' cultural contexts and times.[1] The Bible was written and compiled by humans whose experiences are not our experiences. How they understood the world is much different from how we understand it today. Their world views are not our world views, their cultures are not our culture, the languages they spoke are not our languages. In addition, our scripture is also filtered through the views and experiences of its many translators and interpreters.

Today it is often interpreted by humans differently and contradictorily. None of the people who have written, compiled, translated and interpreted scripture were or are perfect no matter how inspired by God they may have been. Each had or has their own cultural and political influences and personal motivations. No book could come through that centuries-long process, touched by so many fallible humans, without errors and without contradictions. Responsible reading of the Bible needs to take all of these issues into account.

1 Ibid., 37.

Although the Bible is an important word of revelation, it cannot be considered the final word. While I believe we benefit immensely by taking the Bible seriously, I also think it can be at best misleading and at worst dangerous to take it literally. We must reject biblical literalism, which according to Catherine Keller "freezes theology into single meanings,"[1] as well as any doctrine which points to scripture as the only source of revelation.[2] Such approaches to the Bible set the Bible up as an idol and encourage us to be worshippers of the Bible instead of seekers of God.

Most Christians, even those who claim the Bible as the infallible, literal word of God, do not believe everything printed in its pages. Most people would claim slavery to be immoral and evil and yet the author of the letter to the Colossians accepted the institution of slavery with little objection, telling any who were slaves to "obey your earthly masters in everything."[3] Similarly, in the first letter to the Corinthians, Paul makes women subject to men in religious matters.[4] Yet, most people today recognize that women are as intelligent and as much in God's good graces as any man. It seems clear that on these issues, the biblical authors were swayed not by God's love but by cultural influences, influences that are different in our culture today. Thus, in our times, we can reject slavery as well as the subjugation of women as in conflict with the message of love which is the clear fundamental truth of Christianity.

The people who wrote the Bible weren't infallible and the people who read it and preach about it aren't infallible. The Bible should be treasured as an important source of revelation, but also read with a healthy skepticism in order to find the deeper meanings contained inside. Instead of approaching it literally, the Bible can be understood, as McFague does, as a description of the transformational power of God in the lives of a people of a certain time and place. We can then seek to understand the Bible not only in terms

1 Keller, *On the Mystery*, 15.

2 Tillich, *Systematic Theology, Vol. 1*, 34.

3 Colossians 3:22

4 1 Corinthians 14:33-35

of those past lives but also in terms of our own age and culture.[1] As responsible readers of the Bible, we might ask ourselves questions such as the following:

- Who was the real author of the text and when was the text written? Our Christian traditions surrounding the identity of biblical authors and the time the various texts were written often don't reflect more accurate recent biblical research.
- Who was the intended audience of the text and what were they meant to learn from it?
- Was this audience supposed to understand it literally or as an allegory?
- What was the author's culture like and how were they being influenced by that culture?
- How might the author have been trying to influence their culture?
- What was the political situation at the time the text was written?
- What was the personal situation of the author at the time the text was written? What beliefs and biases did that person carry?
- Was the text limited by the scientific understandings of the period? For example, we now know it is physically impossible for the Sun to stop moving (or, perhaps more accurately, for the Earth to stop rotating).[2] Knowing that, what was the author trying to convey by saying such an event happened? We don't need to dismiss the text because of an inaccuracy, but we can take the time to look for the intended message behind the inaccuracy.
- What did the text mean to those who wrote it? What did it mean to those who included it in the Bible? What does it mean to us today?

Despite the inherent problems in reading and understanding them, the Christian scriptures canonized in the Bible have stood

1 McFague, *Models of God*, 43.

2 Joshua 10:13

the test of time as a source of revelation. As problematic as they can often be, they have been found meaningful by millions of people over many centuries.

The Bible is the important testimony of our Christian faith ancestors, telling us of their faith and beliefs and how they interpreted and understood their experiences of God. Whether we believe a biblical story to be literal or allegorical, the critical understanding comes from the message conveyed by the story. These messages don't change based on whether the events told are completely fictitious or whether they happened verbatim. It's all right if the Bible has inconsistencies and factual errors. The Bible is not God. Christians are not supposed to worship the Bible. What's important is finding the revelations of God within its pages. The Bible is a pointer to God, a kind of spiritual map. At its best, it says to us: God's down this path, let me tell you a story about how you can find your way.

The Bible gives us a foundation for our own spirituality. It gives us a common language to talk about God and a connection to millions of Christians throughout history. It gives us a common set of stories that we can use to reflect on our own personal relationships to God, to each other, and to Creation. As a foundational document of Christianity, the Bible, interpreted and understood in light of our own experiences, does not form a definitive source of revelation, but one of many important vehicles that contribute to our search for the ungiven God.

Human Culture and Wisdom. God does not manifest only in Christian realms. For Tillich, Christian theologians use culture as a means of expression, for both confirmation and contradiction of their views, and find within culture the existential questions which theology needs to answer.[1] Social analysis and modern science can help us by poking holes in some concepts of God and opening up the possibilities of other concepts not yet imagined. Human knowledge and insights gained from sciences such as psychology and physics as well as the humanities such as literature can provide

1 Tillich, *Systematic Theology*, Vol. 1, 38.

important illumination into the human condition and our relationship with the Divine.

Further, because God is present with and to all human beings, and all Creation for that matter, it would be exceedingly arrogant of those of us who are Christians to try to claim a monopoly on revelation. We need to learn from those outside Christianity. Other religions also provide sources of revelation, especially the major religions that have stood the test of time.

Religion in general is simply a framework, a set of stories, language, myths, rituals, and doctrines, that allow us to talk about and try to understand God. A particular framework gives us a common base to approach the deeper questions of life. It doesn't matter whether that framework is Christianity, Judaism, Islam, Buddhism, Hinduism, or another religion, but we need to know one framework well or we will only skim along the surface of our spirituality and never be able to go deep enough to truly find God. If we viewed each religion as a different building — one round, one tall, one short, etc. — but only view the outside then we'll define God by the exterior of the building. We need to go into the building and explore. We need to live there ourselves.

We learn not only from those frameworks in which we dwell, but we can learn much from other frameworks as well. They can perhaps show us new ways to understand what is in our own framework. They can help us find tools, such as meditation, that lie forgotten in our own spiritual home but are still vibrant and important in others.

In addition, references to popular culture, another important aspect of the language of the people, can serve as analogy and metaphor to help bridge the gap between theological language and everyday life. Popular culture provides a wealth of useful images for communication. These images invite further reflection by providing well-known cultural reference points and are particularly useful in thinking about how God is or is not reflected in and by human culture. Many of the above mentioned sources of human culture and wisdom will be drawn upon throughout our journey to find the ungiven God.

Creation. Just as God does not manifest solely within Christianity, God does not manifest just in human realms. We can find God within all of Creation, within any aspect of the universe, and within all that exists and that can be perceived by human beings. Sallie McFague uses the world as a metaphor for God's body.[1] This metaphor implies that the body of God consists of more than just Christians and more than just humans.

If we only look, we will find testimony of the Divine in all the corners of Creation. God, as described in the Bible, for example, is often encountered on a mountain top or in a storm cloud. Many people understand God to be revealed in the beauty of nature. In the reds and oranges of the sunset we might find a sense of awe and transcendence that moves us closer to God. In gazing upon a blooming flower we might experience a holy and sacred moment. We might also sometimes become more aware of God in the power of nature, such as a lightening storm, when we sense that there is more to the world around us then we observe. Others might understand God as guiding natural processes such as evolution, bringing some kind of order to what can often seem like chaos.

Certainly, we can use our brains to scientifically explain nature, but our minds are not the only way humans have to analyze and experience Creation. What our hearts, our emotions and feelings tell us are worth considering as well. All aspects of Creation can contribute to our search for the ungiven God, whether they be animals, plants, rocks, gasses, liquids, planets, stars or anything else.

Conclusion. This constructive theological journey we are about to embark upon in search of the ungiven God through creation, human culture and wisdom, scripture, and theology, as filtered by human experience, mostly follows the framework of

1 McFague, *Models of God*, 71.

what is known as liberal theology. The theologian Dorothee Söelle defines three primary premises of liberal theology:[1]

1. Scientific discovery should inform our faith and need not contradict it.
2. All Christian writings, dogmas, and doctrines must be analyzed and questioned and are best understood based on the context of their origin.
3. To be relevant, religion must always be in relationship with the culture that surrounds it.

Söelle also offers two criticisms of liberal theology:[2]

1. An assumption of the separation of church and state can lead to an accommodation to the state rather than critique of state injustice. That is, the church and its theologians may tend to cozy up to secular governmental forces rather than risk being critical of them. We might see this today in the facets of Christianity that embrace capitalism and patriotism without questioning their effects on the oppressed of the world.
2. An emphasis on individualism can cause our theologies to concentrate on the salvation of individual persons and ignore the plight of the masses who live under conditions of hunger, poverty, and oppression.

While our journey will utilize the liberal theological viewpoint as we begin our search for the ungiven God, we will also endeavor not to be trapped by the pitfalls that can accompany this outlook. Along the way we will find that there are many potential sources of the revelation of God's manifestation, all of which are dependent on human experience to receive and interpret. It is through bringing all of these experiences and testimonies of revelation together in

1 Dorothee Söelle, *Thinking About God: An Introduction to Theology,* trans. John Bowden (Harrisburg, PA: Trinity Press International, 1990), 13-15.
2 Ibid., 16-17.

our time and for our context that we might more fully illuminate that which we can't see alone, the ungiven God, the hidden and unknowable God, much like trying to see an elephant in a dark room.

Chapter 1 Discussion Questions

1. What are some of the understandings of God that you have been given? Which of these have you struggled with and why?
2. How has God been revealed in your own life experiences?
3. What do you give authority in your life (for example, your pastor, the Bible, secular media, political figures, family members, science, etc.)? Why?

2 Naughty or Nice

Shaping Our Theology

From an early age, our theology is shaped by a multitude of factors that form the context of our lives. These may include what we are explicitly taught by parents and religious leaders, our experiences, the observations we make of the world around us, and the workings of our culture. It is probably impossible to untangle all of the various factors that contribute to our concept of God.

As we grow and mature, we analyze these teachings, experiences, and observations in a life-long process, testing whether or not they are consistent with the God-concepts that we have compiled along the way. Sometimes we discover that things don't match up. We may come to the realization that our given God doesn't make sense anymore and we either abandon God or go in search of the ungiven God. In these pages I make my own search for the ungiven God and invite the reader to accompany me, hopefully finding this process helpful in their own search. Since this journey will be informed by my personal life experiences it seems wise and necessary to try to relate some of the major factors that I understand as having shaped my faith.

I grew up attending a small town protestant church in the 1970's and 1980's. I have fond memories of my childhood church as it instilled in me a love of and a yearning for God. This church was an important part of my spiritual development as it helped me understand church as a place of loving community. Through its lack of formal membership, in which one was considered part of the church if you attended and professed to be a Christian, it also taught me that one's relationship with God is a personal one and not subject to requirements imposed by other humans.

God was presented as a loving father as well as an all-powerful judge. If you accepted Jesus, God's son, as your savior then you would go to heaven. If you didn't, you would go to hell. The picture of God as an old, wise man with a long, flowing beard and dressed in white flowing robes would not have been out of place. This was an image that unraveled for me, however, as I grew older.

By the time I was leaving home for college this concept of God was losing its cohesiveness. If God was loving then why would he (and God *was* a he) punish perfectly nice people in hell for all of eternity just because they didn't bow down and worship him? If God was all powerful and miracles were real then why would God allow people to suffer so much? I didn't have answers to these and similar questions and the faithful people of my childhood church didn't seem to either. The best answer I could find was an unsatisfactory "we have to have faith." As a result, I drifted away from organized Christianity for about thirteen years, although I maintained a passing interest in religion and spirituality.

The conflicting image of an all-knowing, all-powerful, judging, but also loving God who seemed to act in arbitrary and irrational ways was the concept of a supreme being that I was given in my formative years. At some point, its similarity to another popular image of an all-knowing, bearded old man, who happened to dress in a red suit instead of white robes but who also judged people and then rewarded or punished them accordingly, became all too obvious. My spiritual life since then has been the search for new understandings of the loving God that I had been given and experienced and yet could not reconcile with the Santa-for-adults God image I was also given as a child.

Along the way, I came to realize that, much like Santa declares little children naughty or nice, in the eyes of much of the wider church I was indeed very naughty because I was attracted to other men. All too common is the story of the young man or woman who, in coming to terms with their sexuality, is driven away from a church which rejects anything that deviates from its one "true" way of being, which includes mandatory heterosexuality. Such churches present a corollary image to the Santa-for-adults God: the Everyone-must-be-like-me God of Christian fundamentalism. Those who don't fit the approved mold of action and appearance as determined by these churches — which looks suspiciously like the image of God they project — are not welcome.

In a peculiar twist of fate, accepting myself as a gay man was what brought me back to my Christian faith and a church community, albeit in a more progressive form, where I discovered that there are other ways to think of and understand the mystery we call God. The theological reflections that form this book are deeply influenced by that community, Phoenix Community Church, United Church of Christ, in Kalamazoo, Michigan, and its people. This church has had a profound impact on my life as I sought and continue to seek liberation from the overly simplistic Santa-for-adults God and from the polarizing and oppressing Everyone-must-be-like-me God of Christian fundamentalism.

I first heard of Phoenix Community Church in 1997 as I was in the process of coming out as a gay man. Because of its reputation as a "gay church," I sought out this church while in the midst of learning to accept myself, hoping to meet other LGBT (Lesbian, Gay, Bisexual, and Transgender), or queer people in a safe, non-threatening environment. What I found was a progressive theology that would lead my life in unexpected new directions. I found a church where people were taught that God loves everyone just as they are and that one doesn't need to hold certain beliefs as dictated by the church to be in relationship with God. In finding a loving community of people on their own spiritual journeys but gathered together to question, explore, and be in relationship with each other and with God, I was able to discover God again in my own life.

Phoenix Community Church was founded in 1988 by a small group of people under the leadership of the Revs. Cyril Colonius and Melanie Morrison in response to Rev. Colonius' dismissal from a different church the previous year when it became publicly known that he was a gay man. The name of the church carried significant meaning for those beginning this adventure and resonates with the project of leaving behind our given God in search of the ungiven God:

> The phoenix is a mythological bird that rises out of its own ashes to new life. This Egyptian myth was appropriated by the early Christian church as a symbol of resurrection. The people in Kalamazoo who gathered to form a new church also appropriated this myth as a symbol of our belief that resurrection is possible out of the ashes of discrimination, self-hatred, and oppression.[1]

From its beginning, an important part of the Phoenix Community Church ethos has been forming and being in community with each other. Indeed, the church's mission statement, adopted in 1989 and updated in 2013, reads like a recipe for community living:

> Phoenix is a church community that encourages spiritual growth. Questions are taken seriously, and the people of Phoenix share the struggles and joys of being alive.
>
> All are welcomed at Phoenix, regardless of age, abilities, sex, race, sexual orientation, gender identity and expression. We wish to rejoice in our differences while we affirm our similarities.
>
> At Phoenix, we encourage and celebrate the whole person - mind, body, spirit and imagination. We use new forms of worship that speak to a church community with a variety of beliefs. We attempt to avoid language that is hurtful or exclusive.
>
> The people of Phoenix share good times together and try to support one another during hard times. We do not want to become self-satisfied and complacent, but seek instead to be a life-giving church community that reaches out and welcomes in.

---

1 Melanie Morrison, "How We Believe at Phoenix Community Church, UCC," Phoenix Community Church archives, 1989.

> We believe that the spiritual life cannot be divorced from an active concern for the world. Individually and collectively, we seek to challenge oppression and injustice, and work for peace and the preservation of the environment.
>
> To fulfill our mission, we need the presence of the spirit and the support of one another. We seek to forgive ourselves and each other when we fail, and to accept the responsibility to begin anew.[1]

In addition to its mission as the first church in Kalamazoo, Michigan to provide a welcoming and safe space for queer people, the above mission statement also points to two other important factors in its history and development. First, as a community which gathered in those wounded by unwelcoming churches and strove to offer a place of healing, Phoenix struggled in its early years with the extent to which it could be Christian. Formed by people who had been rejected by more fundamental strands of Christianity, new expressions of faith and new theologies have been needed. Although over the years the church has increasingly embraced Christian language and expression, it continues to recognize the value of questioning our faith traditions. The people of the church also continue to encompass a wide range of religious backgrounds and hold diverse beliefs about and understandings of God, Jesus, and Spirit.

These sentiments can be seen in its expression of core values and beliefs:

Our Core Values:

1. An unconditional welcome to all people
2. Using inclusive, compassionate language
3. An intimate worship experience
4. Providing a safe emotional & physical space
5. Being able to talk about our differences

1 "Our Mission Statement," http://www.phoenixchurch.org/mission.php (accessed 30 May 2016).

Our Core Beliefs:

1. Questions are critical: we don't have all the answers
2. We are called to actively be God's love in the world
3. God speaks to each one of us
4. God / Jesus / Spirit = Love
5. God is still speaking[1]

Secondly, as part of this progressive ethos of questioning, this church has maintained an important commitment to inclusive language. An official church policy calls for the use of language that seeks "to reflect the experience and worth of all persons" and includes "either a balance of male and female images or images that are not gender specific" when referencing God.[2] This policy manifests in various ways. For example, what is commonly known as the "Lord's Prayer" is referred to as the "Disciple's Prayer" and the phrase "Our Mother-Father God" is recited as the beginning of that prayer. Likewise, the word kingdom is commonly replaced by "kin-dom"[3] and the usage of terms such as blind as a synonym for ignorance or white as a synonym for purity is given careful consideration.

Meaningful discussions have taken place on the appropriateness of theological language and its implications, including terms such as sin and salvation. Such terms have often been used by the church in the past not to help people but to scare and control them, thereby causing immense spiritual damage. To heal, it is necessary to carefully consider the offending language to decide whether it can be reclaimed or whether our faith might be better served by finding new language and new expressions.

---

1 "Our Core Values & Beliefs," http://www.phoenixchurch.org/beliefs.php (accessed 30 May 2016).

2 "Inclusive Language," http://www.phoenixchurch.org/inclusive.php (accessed 30 May 2016).

3 "Kin-dom" is a variation of "kingdom" meant to deemphasize the implication of patriarchy found in the word "king" and emphasize the implication of close relationship in the word "kin."

These approaches to faith and community have had a profound effect on my own spiritual journey, both as a long time member and lay leader of the congregation and in my current role as the pastor of the church. The transition from member to pastor was a long time in the making. In late 2004 I attended a workshop on shamanic journeying led by the pastor of Phoenix Community Church at that time. This spiritual practice, which is independent of any particular religious faith, helped me to be more open to the leading of the heart instead of relying solely on the reasoning of the mind and opened me to new possibilities and new ways of experiencing God. When that pastor left the church in early 2005, I found myself organizing and leading worship services while we awaited the hiring of an interim pastor. I began to realize that perhaps God had given me a message and was now pushing me to see that I had also been given the gifts to offer that message to others.

About this same time, I decided to leave my job in the information technology field. The time off while looking for new employment gave me an opportunity for spiritual study that was a true blessing. I devoted a large part of my time to strengthening my relationship with God through reading, Bible study, prayer, and meditation. I reached a new closeness with God that I had never experienced before and began to feel drawn to seminary. Although I wasn't sure exactly to what I was being called, my life circumstances allowed me to begin attending seminary in the fall of 2007, when I enrolled at Chicago Theological Seminary. I graduated with a Master of Arts degree in 2009, having decided that parish ministry was not for me.

However, as the saying goes, God works in mysterious ways. Within a year of completing my studies, Phoenix Community Church experienced another ministerial change and the people of the church asked me to step in as the part time pastor. After a year, the church called me as its settled pastor, in which capacity I continue to serve as of this writing. During my time as the pastor of Phoenix Community Church I returned to seminary and completed a Master of Divinity degree in early 2015.

While much of its theological and cultural commitments have remained fairly consistent, Phoenix Community Church has undergone many changes. The church has dwindled in size after a succession of pastoral changes and today struggles with all the typical issues that small churches deal with. Size, however, does not reflect relevance. Those who remain part of this faith community continue to find it a meaningful place to share their spiritual journeys.

Many people share experiences similar to the people of this church: alienation and rejection by more fundamental strands of Christianity; discontinuity between the images of God given to us as children and our lived experiences of the Divine; and an inability to accept doctrines which contradict science and reason. These types of experiences cause us to either reject the exploration of our spirituality and a relationship with God or they cause us to seek new answers and alternatives to our given God. Indeed, perhaps part of the reason Phoenix Community Church remains small is related to these issues. Past negative experiences of hard-sell fire and brimstone fundamentalism has left many with a disdain for evangelism (which isn't necessarily a bad thing). In addition, those with whom the people of Phoenix Community Church identify are often those who want nothing to do with Christianity because they too have been deeply damaged by churches in the past.

Indeed, all of us are living in an age that is increasingly rejecting the institution of the Christian church and holds religion in general in deep suspicion. Other authors have written eloquently about these trends and what it might mean for the future of the church.[1] What is important is that the old ways of being church are not meeting the spiritual needs of new generations which are more and more undergoing crises of discontinuity between their given God and their life experience.

1 For example, Diana Butler Bass in *Christianity After Religion: The End of Church and the Birth of a New Spiritual Awakening* and Phyllis Tickle in *The Great Emergence: How Christianity Is Changing and Why.*

In response, much of the church has simply held onto their given God all the more tightly, refusing to let go at all costs and resulting in a rise in what is usually named as Christian conservatism or fundamentalism. Fear of change is powerful, but fundamentalism comes not just from a fear of change, but from a fear of the loss of one's world view. It results, I believe, when people fear that the world as they understand it is crumbling around them. If one's given God is questioned then, in some sense, the very fabric of how the world is supposed to work and be understood is also questioned. If there is no new understanding or world view to replace that which is being challenged, it can indeed be frightening and disorienting.

However, clinging to an understanding of God which many people increasingly find irrelevant to their lives results in a loss of trust in the church, which then itself becomes increasingly irrelevant. It is my belief that we must, for Christianity to remain a positive force in this world, trust that God is big enough and robust enough to be questioned. Instead of clinging to our given images of God, we need to let go of our inherited understandings and the world view they engender and seek out the ungiven God, the mysterious, as yet undiscovered God.

My personal faith development has occurred within the contours of these larger cultural religious trends. Phoenix Community Church, which I have described ever so briefly, has deeply influenced my faith and theology and this community has therefore also deeply influenced the following theological reflections. In many places, I will be using the experiences and theology of this church as a basis for my reflections. Of course, my seminary education and my work as a pastor have also been important influences. In fact much of the work contained in this book comes from work I did in seminary or from sermons I've written as an active minister. My own journey in search of the ungiven God has been long and sometimes difficult and it's not over yet. The spiritual journey is a process that never really ends because God is always revealing more to us as we go.

Can those who have experienced the failure of faith and theology in their lives find a new way? Can we ultimately escape the Santa-for-adults God who decides who is naughty or nice? Can we get out from under the impositions of the Everyone-be-like-me God? If so, then who or what is God today to Phoenix Community Church, to queer people, to all those who struggle with their current understandings of God, and to me? The so-called decline of the church in our culture may very well save Christianity in the long run if it means that we stop and take the time to ask questions such as these.

It is my wish that in these pages, we might find some possible alternatives to consider. I do not expect to offer definitive answers. Such a thing would be impossible. However, I hope the reader will be encouraged and inspired to seek out new ideas and other progressive Christians in their own search for the ungiven God.

Chapter 2 Discussion Questions

1. In what ways have you experienced the Santa-for-adults God or the Everyone-must-be-like-me God?
2. If you grew up in a faith tradition, what are some of the beliefs that you were taught that hold true for you today? Are there other beliefs that no longer ring true?
3. What religious words or concepts do you find troublesome (such as sin, salvation, etc.)? Why?[1]

---

1 For a more in depth discussion of the language of Christianity, a good resource is Marcus Borg's book "Speaking Christian: Why Christian Words Have Lost Their Meaning and Power -- And How They Can Be Restored."

3 The Electrifying Gravity of Love

Thoughts on God

Burns, Morisette, or Freeman: Old Metaphors

When trying to understand this mystery we call God we often fill in the blanks of what we don't know with projections of what we do know. Because it is often easiest, and perhaps most natural, we tend to make God in our own image and attribute to God the characteristics of an idealized human. For example, in a warrior culture, God becomes the ultimate warrior. In a culture that values wisdom God becomes wise. If we value money, God becomes a capitalist. If we place family in high esteem, then God might come to be understood as a father or mother with whatever stereotypical attributes those archetypes carry in our culture, such as judge or nurturer. In these ways, we begin to expect God to respond as we might expect a human being to respond. God becomes the epitome of what we as humans want to be.

If we are to make God in the image of a person, where does that image come from? In popular culture we have seen various portrayals of God such as George Burns in the 1977 movie *Oh, God!* Or Alanis Morisette in the 1999 movie *Dogma.* Or Morgan Freeman in the 2003 movie *Bruce Almighty.* If God is like a person, then which person? Is God more like an old white man, a young white woman, or a middle aged black man? The fact that the first three images of God in film that I thought of are all comedies is, perhaps, a reminder that we need to keep a sense of humor. Our attempts at pinning down God's nature can sometimes be quite comical and at other times downright dangerous. However, despite the problems in personifying God, we will not stop doing so anytime soon because the image of the idealized human is so familiar to us.

This familiarity is one of the reasons that theologian Sallie McFague believes such personal models for God are so valuable.[1] We as humans have a deep yearning to know God and personifications are the language of the people. They are known to us and thus comfortable and reassuring. Personified images are the analogies which we can know, understand, and relate to most readily.

However, personified images can be as dangerous as they can be profoundly useful. Such images of God are always in danger of being twisted by humanity for its own purposes. God as warrior can be used to justify the use of violence. A capitalist God can be used to affirm that the rich are more deserving than the poor and justify continued economic oppression. The father God can be used to reinforce the subjugation of women while propping up patriarchal power structures. Whenever we perceive of God as an idealized human being, that image is forever in danger of becoming a parody of the ideal human self. God is forever in danger of becoming the Santa-for-adults God or the Everyone-must-be-like-me God.

These personifications too often become attempts to enforce conformity while building the power of those who look most like the particular image of God. For example, George Burns portraying God as an elderly white man subtly reinforces white supremacy as well as oppressive patriarchal systems. Mary Daly rightly points out that "if God is male, then the male is God."[2] Likewise, if God is white, then the white (man) is also God. Portrayals of God as woman or as black such as those by Morissette or Freeman can help disturb, but probably not completely correct, such harmful projections. They may also simply change the external characteristics of the Everyone-must-be-like-me God and not correct the harmful aspects that such a concept of God represents.

1 McFague, *Models of God*, 82.

2 Mary Daly, *Beyond God the Father: Toward a Philosophy of Women's Liberation* (Boston: Beacon Press, 1985), 19.

Many people, such as queer people or women, have had direct negative experiences with personifications of God as the ideal human. This Everyone-must-be-like-me God has often been used to condemn and ostracize persons with a non-conforming gender or sexuality (i.e. those who are not male and heterosexual). For these people, any God concept that attempts to queer or break down the boundaries of the Everyone-must-be-like-me God is helpful. McFague argues that the personification of God is not the problem, but the problem instead lies in the types and limited scope of the personifications that we choose. She believes that we need new and more appropriate metaphors and proposes metaphors of mother, lover, and friend to complement the traditional metaphor of God as father.[1]

While I would agree with McFague that new and more appropriate metaphors are needed, I would argue that any personification of God carries the potential of recreating the Everyone-must-be-like-me God and continuing its history of damage and condemnation. It might be best in the long run if we could wean ourselves away from such personifications completely, however difficult that may be. Indeed, it probably will not be entirely possible because, as already noted above, personified images are often the most familiar and the ones we can relate to the easiest. Even if we cannot rid ourselves of potentially harmful personifications of God, we can use multiple metaphors as McFague suggests so that no particular one takes precedence. However, just as we can try to balance our personifications of God with alternative personified images, it is equally important, I believe, to also explore new non-personified metaphors for God as well. If we are searching for a God that is unknown and hidden, perhaps it makes more sense to look in arenas that are not so familiar and attempt to find metaphors that can say something about our experience of and relationship to God without identifying God as some kind of super human being.

1 McFague, *Models of God*, 19.

Paul Tillich also warns against the personification of God.[1] For Tillich, God must participate in every human life to be God, but God could not do this if God were a person. If God cannot actually be a person then it makes sense to question the usefulness of talking about God as if God were a person. Granted, Christian tradition holds that humans are created in the image of God, but this doesn't necessarily require us to think of God as performing a human role such as father or mother. There are other ways in which humans might be understood to be images of God and we will explore some of those in the next chapter.

To talk of God using a personal model is to risk creating God in the image of humans. Perhaps there are non-human metaphors and analogies that might open up new understandings of God. If we are to talk of God as something other than a person, then paying attention to language will be important. Tillich's own language is a product of his time in that even after asserting that God is not a person, he continues to refer to God as a he. If God is not a person, then God is not a he or even a she. This is a critical theological issue that needs to be addressed to counter the dangers of the personification of God. A commitment to balanced non-gendered language is needed and sexed pronouns will have to go, as will words such as kingdom and lord, which turn God into a male being. Seeking alternative language is necessary if we are serious about avoiding the problems of personification when it enshrines a particular set of human characteristics as Godly and thus, perhaps unwittingly, creates the Everyone-must-be-like-me God.

The language problem does not stop there, however. Even the word God is problematic. Although it is probably as sexless as a sexed word can become, it still carries its unspoken counterpart, Goddess, along with it, silently reinforcing that God is not female but male. No matter how hard I might want God to be a sexless term, the image that lingers at the shadowy margins of my consciousness is the picture of the old white man with a beard. In our churches and in our Christian liturgies, I'm not sure there is much

1 Tillich, *Systematic Theology, Vol. 1*, 245.

we can do to address that problem in the short term. But, we can certainly begin to introduce new language alongside the old. We can begin to try out new names for God while re-emphasizing old names such as Creator or Sustainer.

The Bible offers many different names and descriptions for God, some personifications and some not. Other belief systems also recognize the complexity of God. Islam gives ninety-nine names for God with a hundredth name being hidden from humankind. Hinduism honors many deities, each representing a different aspect of God. Taoism recognizes God as something formless and eternal, that can't be named by humankind. Perhaps it is in this multiplicity of names and images that we might find a more complete picture of God, each one forming a piece of the puzzle.

I will continue by striving to avoid personifications in general, using the term Divine Presence to point toward God, all the while remembering that the ungiven Divine Presence cannot be fully captured or defined. In that way, it might also be pointed to as the Queering Divine Presence, always uncontainable and "so extreme that it dissolves" human constructed boundaries and categories.[1] Being uncontainable, we should not be surprised should the Queering Divine Presence present us with mystery, confusion, and even contradiction as we attempt to contain and know it.

The Power You're Supplying, It's Electrifying: New Metaphors

If the Divine Presence is not a person, then how else can it be understood? If the language of theology is to be metaphor and analogy, then to what can we compare our experience of the Divine so that we might begin to understand it? Here are some ways in which I have experienced the Divine Presence which are not personifications but might also be pieces of the puzzle we are trying to

1 Patrick Cheng, *Radical Love: An Introduction to Queer Theology* (New York: Seabury Books, 2011), 44. The word queer in this statement is not meant to personify God by referring to queer people, but is meant to imply the transgression of human imposed boundaries.

put together. This is, of course, in no way meant to be an exhaustive list. Included are some of the places that the same concepts can be found in the Bible:

- God as **love**: God lives in us as love (1 John 4:12). Nothing can separate us from the love of God (Romans 8:38-39). The fruit of the Spirit is love (Galatians 5:22). God is love and love is from God (1 John 4:7-8).
- God as **peace**: Peace is found through Jesus (John 14:27, 16:33). Life and peace are found in the Spirit (Romans 8:6). The fruit of the Spirit is peace (Galatians 5:22).
- God as **within all things**: The realm of God is within us (Luke 17:21). God is within all things, all things are within God.
- God as **the source of creation**: All things originate in God (Ephesians 3:9, Colossians 1:16).
- God as **kindness**: Love is kind (1 Corinthians 13:4). The fruit of the Spirit is kindness (Galatians 5:22).
- God as **rock, fortress, and refuge**: God is the solid foundation which sees us through the uncertainties of life (Psalm 18:1-2).
- God as **abundance**: God is my shepherd, I shall not want (Psalm 23:1). God will supply what we need (Matthew 6:25-34). This is not meant to imply any kind of "prosperity gospel." The Bible is also clear about the dangers of wealth (Matthew 19:24).
- God as **welcoming**: God is waiting for us to knock, ask, search and God will open the door, take us in, and give freely (Matthew 7:7-11).
- God as **forgiveness**: Be forgiving and God will forgive us (Matthew 6:14). We must be right with the world to be right with God.
- God as **justice**: Jesus rebukes the religious leaders for neglecting issues of justice (Luke 11:42). The Bible shows a

These are all aspects we attribute to the Divine; they are not metaphors or images - of which there are many in the Bible & in all holy writings / wisdom

deep appreciation for justice for those in need such as the poor and abused.

- God as **found in the quiet of the soul**: The soul waits in silence to find the salvation and hope of God (Psalm 62:1,5).
- God as **eternal**: God always was and will always be (John 1:1-5). There is something in God that transcends the physical and speaks to the eternal-ness of life (John 4:13-14).
- God as **life-giving**: God, through each of us, is a life-giving force, a supplier of "living water" (John 7:38).
- God as **inclusive**: The good news of God is a great joy for all people (Luke 2:10).

I would like to explore more deeply one of these images which I think also incorporates most of the others. As a starting point, we might consider Phoenix Community Church's core belief that the Divine Presence communicates or in some way speaks to each one of us, which is also echoed in the United Church of Christ affirmation that "God is Still Speaking." This claim is reflective of Tillich's assertion that to be the Divine Presence, it *must* participate in every life. Not just some lives, but every life. We have also already said the Divine Presence is queering, uncontainable, and boundary-breaking, which implies transformation and adaptation. So what non-personified metaphor or image of God speaks to each of us, participating in our lives, and yet is uncontainable and boundary-breaking, creating transformation within us while helping us adapt to ever-changing contexts?

I would propose love as an image of the Divine Presence that meets these criteria. It is not only a traditional concept (many theologians and the biblical record concur that the Divine Presence is love[1]), but makes a fitting and important metaphor that avoids personification of the Divine. We avoid personification because we

1 For example, see Cheng, *Radical Love*, ix; Catherine Keller, *God and Power: Counter-Apocalyptic Journeys* (Minneapolis: Fortress Press, 2005), 151; Sallie McFague, *A New Climate For Theology: God, the World,*

are not asserting that the Divine Presence loves but that the Divine Presence *is* love. Love itself is a force present in all life and at its most basic levels involves transformation and adaptation.

Where might we be led if we took this assertion that the Divine Presence is love more seriously? Tillich offers the insight that love has to do with separation and reunion.[1] One element of love is the desire to be united and in relationship with that which we love so we might be fulfilled. As love, the Divine Presence is the force which works to bring "every creature" which is "separated or disrupted" to fulfillment in the unity of the Divine.[2] As love, then, the Divine Presence is more than an emotion. It is an active and radical force that works to break down the walls that separate us from each other and from the Divine and therefore enables reunion, a coming together of creature and divinity. It makes possible the finding of wholeness.

Love as the Divine Presence, in this sense, might be likened to the force of gravity, which acts to pull two separated bodies together and hold them there in relationship with each other. Love exerts a pull on creation, calling and luring it toward wholeness, "our fullest becoming."[3] In this metaphor, the Divine Presence becomes the gravitational force of love and its pull toward wholeness represents how the Divine acts in our lives. The emotional component of love comes from the awareness of this growing wholeness within us.[4]

The Divine Presence as the gravitational energy of love works as a felt but unseen force making us whole. When we are estranged from the Divine, it pulls us toward reunion. When we are estranged from each other, it pulls us toward reunion. When we are estranged from Creation, it pulls us toward reunion. Whenever we fall short of our full potential as human beings, whenever our lives are broken or fractured, the gravitational energy of love seeks to pull us

and Global Warming (Minneapolis: Fortress Press, 2008), 50; Tillich, *Systematic Theology, Vol. 1*, 279; 1 John 4:8

1 Tillich, *Systematic Theology, Vol. 1*, 280.

2 Ibid., 281.

3 Keller, *God and Power*, 30.

4 Tillich, *Systematic Theology, Vol. 1*, 279-280.

back into the people we were created to be, to make us whole once more. To submit ourselves to this force, to be in relationship with and follow the ways of the Divine Presence, is to submit ourselves to love, to give ourselves over to the uniting power of love, and to love the Divine, our neighbors, and ourselves as we are loved by the Divine. In this way we begin to live in harmony with the Divine, the force of love that permeates the universe, and are united in love. When this happens, when the gravitational force of love has united us with the Divine Presence, another person, or Creation, we feel it as the emotion of love, the warmth and contentment that we often associate with love, the feeling that all is as it should be.

The Divine Presence as love not only lures us to wholeness, to the realization of our potential in the reunion with the Divine, but it provides the life-giving energy that allows us to make that journey. Taking a clue from John Travolta's character in the movie *Grease*, who sings "the power you're supplying, it's electrifying!" to his romantic interest, we might also think of the Divine Presence as not just a gravitational love but as an electrifying power of love.

Some of the same descriptors we might use for electricity we can also use for love and the Divine Presence, such as intangible and powerful. Electricity and love have no form, but have the potential, the capacity, to do great work, which is the scientific definition of energy. The Divine Presence also has great power. It may not always be obvious, but it is always there, ready to be tapped into. Love and electricity aren't necessarily easy to understand or predict. We don't always understand exactly how the Divine Presence works, either. Is the Divine sitting back directing our lives or is it more like a creative love energy, waiting to be connected to in the proper ways? If connected properly, electricity is very beneficial. If we are connected to the Divine Presence appropriately, we will benefit in profound ways that will transcend our ability to understand as we are energized and pulled toward wholeness.

Electricity flows through us and around us and is found in many different incarnations. For example, it might be experienced as uncontainable lightening, as current in wires, or as the static charge that our bodies might hold. Love, too, is within and all around us and can be found in different forms such as the loving act of a stranger, the love of a friend or the sensual love of a sexual partner. Likewise, the Divine Presence which is the gravitational, electrifying force of love can be found everywhere and in many incarnations.

You can't physically touch love or electricity but they exist everywhere. This is the Divine Presence as omnipresent. The Divine is in us and we are in the Divine. Nothing exists that doesn't contain the Divine and that isn't contained within the Divine. The Divine is in animals, plants, and even rocks, furniture, and other inanimate objects. The Divine is everywhere. Our very souls are part of the Divine Presence, which surrounds us every day, all day and is in the very fiber of our being.

Just as electricity allows the heart to distribute life-force to our physical bodies, we also see in literature that electricity is sometimes understood as life-giving. For example, the monster in the novel *Frankenstein* by Mary Shelley was animated or given life with electricity. The electrifying gravity of love that is the Divine Presence, which is infinite, uncontainable, and unconditionally available to all of Creation, is also that which gives us life. It is what makes us whole and gives us belonging and meaning.

Messy Incarnation: Unity and Multiplicity

Wholeness could be understood as achieving one-ness with the Divine and thus becoming who the Divine Presence intends us to be. However, when we speak of achieving union with the Divine Presence, we need to be cautious. Unity has many good things going for it. Humans often need some sense of unity to accomplish tasks and to work together with minimal acrimony toward common goals. Unity can create meaning through a sense of belonging to something important and it can provide support in times of trouble.

However, human ideas of unity can also cause serious problems and lead to the belief that to have unity, humans must also be *one*: looking, thinking, and acting the same as each other in an idealized manner. The ideal to which we must all conform is represented by the Everyone-must-be-like-me God and is dictated by those at the top of the religious hierarchical and patriarchal power structures. Christianity has not only traditionally applied such models of same-ness to followers, but has applied them even to the *One God*, a more traditional name for the Everyone-must-be-like-me God, who must also strictly adhere to the doctrines of the established Christian power structures.

That is, to establish the Divine Presence as the One (and only true) God, as Theologian Laurel Schneider points out, it requires that any non-orthodox "appearances or claims about divinity" be rejected as false.[1] To maintain the absolute oneness, or purity, of God, everything that doesn't fit in our concept of the One God must be demonized and ostracized.[2] Therefore, if the One God, for example, only blesses heterosexual relationships, as so many people claim, then those who are gay or lesbian or bisexual don't fit the approved model of humanity and they must be demonized and ostracized. They represent an ambiguity that cannot be tolerated because it challenges the very existence of the One God.

The logic of oneness attempts to make everything dualistic, true or false, right or wrong.[3] We crave certainty and security and try to achieve it through making everything orderly and making everything conform to one system or one way of being. But these

1 Laurel Schneider, *Beyond Monotheism: A Theology of Multiplicity* (London and New York: Routledge, 2008), 79. I am using "God" here because I will argue that the "One God" is, like the Santa Claus God, inadequate. The One God is not the same as the proposed concept of the Divine Presence.

2 The anthropologist Mary Douglas claimed that for humans the "quest for purity is pursued by rejection" and "purity is the enemy of change, of ambiguity and compromise." Mary Douglas, *Purity and Danger* (London and New York: Routledge Classics, 2002), 199-200.

3 Schneider, 86.

visions of oneness deny our real experiences. Life's unique manifestations and happenings often transgress the rules and categories to which we expect the world to adhere. For example, we tend to view gender as a binary. We are either male or female. But, this ignores an entire spectrum of experiences in between, causing the rejection of many whose emotional and physical realities don't match the approved gender duality, such as intersex and transgender people. Our ideas of oneness often deny the complexity of life by trying to make everything simple. But life is filled with contradictions.[1]

Yet, despite the dangerous way the concept has manifested in our doctrines and practices, we cannot deny the importance of oneness in the Christian tradition, whether it be the One God or the oneness of its followers. In the gospel of John, Jesus prays at the last supper that the disciples and all that follow them will be one.[2] The recounting of Jesus' words in this instance are perhaps intended by the author of the Gospel of John to primarily address a community isolated from their Jewish culture and encourage unity among them in the manner of helping and supporting each other.[3] However, we might also contemplate whether Jesus' words are a suggestion of something deeper, such as the realization of a deeper connection at the core of our very being. Regardless, the typical human understanding of oneness as same-ness is problematic when applied to human beings and does not fit with our experience of life or the Divine Presence. We need a new way to think of being one.

In Christianity, the incarnation of Jesus opens up other, more flexible ways to think of being one. For Schneider, incarnation is a serious challenge to the logic of oneness and creates the possibility of a logic of multiplicity.[4] The One God is untouchable, static and unaffected by the messiness of life, but the incarnation seems

1 Ibid., 83.

2 John 17:20-23.

3 Robert Goss talks about the isolation of the community addressed by the gospel of John but doesn't specifically comment on these words from chapter 17. See Robert E. Goss, "John," in *The Queer Bible Commentary*, eds. Deryn Guest et al., 548-565 (London: SCM Press, 2006), 549-550.

4 Schneider, 139.

to be a dent in the armor of that inflexible oneness. The Divine Presence, in manifesting as a human through the incarnation, does something new by becoming touchable, changeable, and intimately involved in the messiness of life.

The resurrection creates another dent in the logic of oneness. Part of the promise of resurrection is that the Divine Presence will come again — over and over again. The incarnation of the Divine Presence as Jesus didn't end with his death, but Christianity asserts that Jesus continues to live and be personally relevant in our lives. The resurrection declares that the incarnation was not a one-time thing but is an ongoing event. The resurrection affirms that the Divine Presence continues to be involved in the physicality of our existence.

If we accept this assertion, the Divine Presence dwells within our body-and-soul selves — *all* of our body-and-soul selves. Catherine Keller affirms this fleshiness of the Divine Presence, stating that the incarnation was not just a single event but is "always and everywhere taking place, and always differently."[1] Death does not hold the Divine Presence down, but it is constantly manifesting in this world and in us, constantly becoming multiple, not just in the three of the Trinity but in the infinite differences of Creation. Every person, every animal, every plant, and every rock are all manifestations of the Divine.

God manifests in us in our uniqueness, in what Schneider calls the in-exchangeability of the human.[2] We are each uniquely created, each representing a story, a set of experiences and emotions that cannot be replaced by any other. We each experience the Divine Presence in unique and in-exchangeable ways. There is an infinite uniqueness to the incarnation of the Divine Presence in Creation that denies the logic of oneness. And yet, in that infinite uniqueness there is also an infinite connectedness, which represents the truth of oneness.

---

1 Keller, *On the Mystery*, 52.

2 Schneider, 165.

If we just talked of *the many* manifestations of the Divine Presence it may leave open the impression that the parts are unrelated instances. However, Schneider develops the language of multiplicity when talking of this many faceted oneness of the Divine Presence in order to imply a connectedness and dependency. The parts of a multiplicity help to form each other.[1] The numerous and even infinite separate instances or incarnations that constitute the multiplicity of the Divine Presence are neither completely separate nor completely the same. They can only exist as unique manifestations which co-constitute each other. That is, each unique part needs every other unique part in order to form a whole. Neither absolute separateness nor absolute oneness make sense in the context of Divine multiplicity. It is the underlying co-creating, co-forming connection that makes us one. This connection is the Divine Presence, the queering, electrifying gravity of love. The wholeness toward which the Divine Presence pulls all of Creation is not the false logic of oneness that brooks no ambiguity or contradiction but an essential oneness of being that exists in multiplicity. This is a oneness that connects the multiplicity of manifestations of the Divine at the very core of their being without changing their uniqueness. In fact, to force a same-ness in people would be to disparage the Divine that is manifest in them.

Instead of the untouchable One God that sits above and beyond, the Divine Presence is involved in the messiness and complexity of life, in all of life's differences. We might think of manifestations of the Divine as waves, each unique, different sizes and shapes, moving at different speeds, and with different experiences.[2] Perhaps some encounter rocks or shorelines and some not. These are waves that are constantly forming and reforming, dying and resurrecting. Yet all of these infinitely unique waves are of the

1 Ibid., 142.

2 This wave metaphor is a variation of and inspired by Marjorie Suchocki's use of water as a metaphor for God: Marjorie Hewitt Suchocki, *In God's Presence: Theological Reflections on Prayer* (St. Louis, Missouri: Chalice Press, 1996), 4-5.

same body of water. In their complexity and difference, there is still an underlying oneness.

Similarly, Sallie McFague uses the metaphor of an ecological unity where "the whole is nothing but each of the parts doing its own thing, while the particular parts depend for their existence on the whole"[1] and "the whole cannot be sustained apart from the health of the parts."[2] In a forest, for example, many different trees, plants, and animals each play their particular part in making the forest a living thing. All of these smaller parts of the forest are unique and yet dependent on the forest as a whole for their existence. Each is unique but part of an underlying oneness, as each unique human is a part of the multiplicity of the Divine Presence.

We might also consider the apostle Paul's image of the body of Christ in one Spirit, where the body is not just Christ's believers but all of Creation.[3] Each part of the body is unique and plays its important part. We need the nose to smell and the eyes to see. If the body was all nose, it would not be able to see, or hear, or touch, or taste. And yet the body is one even in the uniqueness of its parts. So too the Divine Presence is one even in the uniqueness of its parts, affirming that in wholeness we remain complex and unique while of one body, the body of Christ, the body of Creation. Anyone who has ever been traumatized by the Everyone-must-be-like-me God can be reassured that they are manifestations of the Divine as they are and need not be concerned about conforming to a false model of same-ness.

Indeed, the Divine Presence cannot be found in utopian visions of same-ness. Instead, it must be found in the complexities and uniqueness of life, pulling us toward wholeness, which is the realization of a oneness, a connection, at the core of our being that rejoices in the in-exchangeability of each individual and particular incarnation. The Divine Presence is found in love, which is felt

1 McFague, *A New Climate*, 52.
2 Ibid., 150.
3 Patrick Cheng, *From Sin to Amazing Grace: Discovering the Queer Christ* (New York: Seabury Books, 2012), 122. See also 1 Corinthians 12:12-26.

in the growing awareness of this divine interconnectedness, our reunion with the Divine Presence.

Divine Mathematics: The Trinity

The divine *we* of creation and the Christian doctrine of the Trinity, according to Catherine Keller, also suggest the possibility of a divine multiplicity.[1] Unfortunately, the Trinity is a concept for which there are many attempted explanations and very little understanding. For some, the Trinity is integral to their spirituality. For others, it might amount to nothing more than a confusing curiosity. However, I believe we can find important insights in the idea of the Divine Presence as Trinity.

When learning mathematics as children we are taught that $1 + 1 + 1 = 3$. But in trinitarian mathematics, $1 + 1 + 1 = 1$. In the mathematics of divine multiplicity we might expand this equation into $1 + 1 + 1 = 1 = \infty$ (infinity). How are we to understand these seeming contradictions? The Trinity hints at how we might make sense of a divine mathematics that does not seem logical. Of course, its illogicalness would seem to be the point. The Trinity is itself a mystery as well as a reflection on the Divine Presence's true relational nature.[2] The Trinity does not fit neatly into the logic of the One God but more rightly belongs to the Divine Presence which embraces and celebrates contradiction and ambiguity in all of its glorious particularity.

Tillich proposes that the number three in the Trinity is entirely irrelevant. For him, the point of the Trinity is to address the "problem of the unity between ultimacy and concreteness."[3] This is the problem of the incarnation: how can the transcendent divine (ultimacy) become particular flesh (concreteness), not only in Jesus but in any of the infinitely unique, co-constituting fleshy incarnations implied by the logic of multiplicity? Of course, in the logic of the One God, the Trinity is limited to three. It is boxed in

1 Keller, *On the Mystery*, 64. See also Genesis 1:26.

2 Cheng, *Radical Love*, 56.

3 Tillich, *Systematic Theology, Vol. 1*, 228.

and contained because we can't let the One God become unmanageable. But, the three of the Trinity doesn't matter if the Trinity is understood as a metaphor for multiplicity. Indeed, even in the three of the Trinity we can find infinite multiplicity.

In his explanation of hope, which seems directly relatable to the three aspects of the Trinity, James Evans names three dimensions of hope in African American theology: the cosmic, the collective, and the personal.[1] The cosmic represents the universal, hope available to all. The collective represents the communal, the hope of the many in relationship as one community. The personal represents the hope of the body-spirit unity.

These three dimensions of hope, the universal, collective, and body-spirit, express the multiplicity of hope, infinite manifestations of hope in three dimensions. Hope is also part of the very nature of the Divine Presence as the electrifying gravity of love. In the turmoil of our lives, the trust that the Divine is pulling us toward wholeness and infusing us with life-giving energy, gives us hope. Although it is not always easy to accept this hope, it is an essential part of our experience of the Divine and as such it is no surprise that the three dimensions of hope can be seen as well in the concept of the Trinity, which is the Divine Presence, Jesus the Christ, and the Holy Spirit.

The Divine Presence itself becomes the cosmic, which is revealed to us in the awe-inspiring beauty of a sunset or the fearful beauty of a lightning storm, and is a transcendent power encompassing all of Creation. Jesus the Christ becomes the collective, the face of the other, the incarnation of the Divine over and over again in every human and in every aspect of Creation, the electrifying power of love that runs through us all. Jesus becomes the reminder of the Divine Presence within our neighbors and calls out to us for justice and love in our relationships. The Holy Spirit becomes the personal, the Divine Presence within us, the electrifying gravity of love that lives within us personally and that pulls us outward to relationship with the cosmic and the collective. Thus the Trinity,

---

1 Evans, 179-180.

when understood together as the infinite cosmos, the innumerable other, and the limitless depths of the personal, reveals itself to be a symbol of infinite multiplicity in relationship.

The infinite relationships of the Divine Presence represented by the Trinity are a "continual flow of giving and receiving, of sharing, of living in one another, of counting on one another."[1] Yet, being in relationship, this multiplicity still maintains its oneness in the essence of our being. The Trinity is a divine mathematics founded on contradiction that demands we know ourselves, each other, and all of Creation as one interconnected, inseparable, in-exchangeable, infinite multiplicity.

We are not bound by the images of the Santa-for-adults God or the Everyone-must-be-like-me God. In searching for the unknowable, hidden Divine Presence we can turn to other metaphors and concepts. I have proposed understanding the Divine Presence as the electrifying gravity of love that pulls us toward wholeness, a celebration of the multiplicity of Creation which realizes its essential oneness. This is a Divine Presence that is profoundly queering because it knows no boundaries and cannot be contained within the language of our concepts of divinity. The best we can do is to continually seek to be in relationship with the Divine Presence in its cosmic, collective and personal forms, in all of its infinite incarnations. And what is more relational than love, the profound foundation of the multiple oneness of the Divine Presence?

---

1 McFague, *A New Climate*, 165.

Chapter 3 Discussion Questions

1. Which images of the Divine Presence resonate with you?
2. What resonates with you in combining gravity and electricity as analogies for the Divine Presence? What concerns you about understanding the Divine as the electrifying gravity of love?
3. How have your images of the Divine changed over your lifetime?
4. In what ways do you see the Divine Presence in people and/or nature?

4 In Our Image

Thoughts on Humanity

We've Fallen and Can't Get Up: The Human Situation

Viktor Frankl, the founder of the school of psychology known as Logotherapy, believed that humanity's primary drive in life is a desire to find meaning. According to Frankl, the spiritual dimension of the human is what separates us from animals and is where this need to find meaning originates.[1] He understood religion as humanity's search for an ultimate meaning.[2] Indeed, it seems clear that when we seek a higher power while pondering the mysteries of life, part of the question we are really asking in our search for the Divine Presence is: who are we? And, why are we? What does it mean to be human? We not only want knowledge of the Divine Presence that we sense at work in the universe but we also want to know our place in the universe and how we relate to that Presence. We seek an ultimate meaning in our lives.

It should come as no surprise, then, that some of our foundational Christian stories seek to address this very question of an ultimate meaning, attempting to answer the questions of who and why we are while discovering the nature of our relationship to the Divine Presence. In fact, the Bible begins with not one but two creation stories, followed by the story of *The Fall* of humanity, all

1 Viktor E. Frankl, *The Doctor and The Soul*, trans. Richard and Clara Winston (New York: Alfred A. Knopf Inc., 1969), x.

2 Viktor E. Frankl, *Man's Search For Ultimate Meaning* (Cambridge, MA: Perseus Publishing, 2000), 17.

of which seek to explore who we are as human beings especially and particularly in relation to the Divine Presence.[1]

The first creation story tells of the Divine Presence creating the universe in seven days.[2] The Divine speaks and the elements of the universe spring forth. Humanity is created in the image of the Divine on the sixth day as caretakers of the world. Seeing what has been made, the Divine Presence declares it very good and rests on the seventh day.

The second creation story tells a slightly different version of the origins of humanity.[3] It explores the relationship of humanity and the Divine Presence through the story of the Garden of Eden. The first human being is brought to life from out of the dust and dirt by the breath of the Divine in order to live in and take care of the garden. After a companion being is created, the tale then continues with what is often known as the story of *The Fall*,[4] in which these archetypal first people, known to us as Adam and Eve, eat fruit that was forbidden to them and are kicked out of the utopian garden.

These foundational stories invite us to ponder the nature of humanity and our relationship with the Divine. However, for many people, these stories are also suspect because they have been used to condemn queer people and women. Some point to Adam and Eve as a model of divinely approved heterosexuality, supposing that their creation as companions for each other represents the one and only model of relationship that the Divine Presence intends. Others have pointed to Adam and Eve as proof that women are subject to men because Eve was created after Adam and derived from his * rib. These are examples of how easily we can fall into the trap of interpreting scriptures to support our personal biases.

These stories say absolutely nothing about homosexuality. Affirming a male-female relationship does not automatically negate same-sex relationships. As has been pointed out by others, to be

1 Genesis 1-3
2 Genesis 1:1-2:4a
3 Genesis 2:4b-25
4 Genesis 3

* What are the creation stories of the ancient peoples before the Hebrews? Babylonians

a commentary on same-sex relationships there would need to be a third character in the story so that the possibility of such a relationship could be addressed. There is nothing in this story to be learned about homosexuality, but there is much food for thought about the nature of humans in general and our relationship to the Divine Presence.

As far as the equality of the sexes, the first creation story tells us that humans are created in the image of the multiplicity of the Divine Presence ("in *our* image"), stating that male and female were created together: "in the image of God he created them; male and female he created them."[1] This passage implies that male and female are complements that co-constitute an image of the Divine Presence.

Although traditionally the second creation story has been understood to say that a male human ("adam" in Hebrew) was created first from "the dust of the ground" (adamah),[2] the original Hebrew isn't really specifying that this first being was of the male gender. Instead, "adam" might better be translated as an earth-creature with an unspecified gender. To create a companion for the earth-creature, the Divine Presence splits the creature in two, and man and woman are brought into existence. Seen in this light we once again have the implication of human genders as complementary to one another rather than subservient. Further, although the woman in some translations is referred to as the man's helper, this does not imply subservience either. The Hebrew word for helper is elsewhere used in the Bible to refer to the Divine Presence as humanity's helper but this certainly is not meant to say that the Divine Presence is subservient to humanity. If anything, calling the woman a helper might be understood to imply that the woman is more capable than the man.

The story of the Fall, where Adam and Eve are evicted from the Garden of Eden, has also been quite controversial due its giving rise to the doctrine of original sin which is often used as evidence

1 Genesis 1:26-27

2 Genesis 2:7

of humans as inherently evil. For some, this doctrine has been used to intimidate and scare by eating away at their self-esteem and convincing them that their only hope is to turn blindly to the institution of the church. Not surprisingly, those who understand themselves to be the good creation of the Divine Presence find a disturbing discontinuity in this perspective. Queer people know how damaging it is to be labeled evil at the very core of one's identity. Thus, the concept of original sinfulness understood as inherent evil looks suspect to queer people whose deepest expressions of love have in the past been labeled by the church as sinful, "intrinsically disordered" and "contrary to the natural law."[1]

Based on the history of abuse, it is tempting to simply dismiss these foundational stories. However, because they maintain a prominent position in Christian tradition, it is important to seek new understandings of their insights into human nature while still rejecting their hurtful and oppressive interpretations.

One problem is that too many people try to understand these stories literally. They are clearly not meant to relate actual historical events. Science, for example, clearly demonstrates that our universe has evolved in a process that has taken place over millions of years and not just seven days. Instead, these stories are analogies or metaphors. They might even be called myths. Our culture has come to understand the word myth to mean a story that is "false," but in fact a myth is a story not meant to relate historical events but to convey some deeper truth. Myths are wisdom teachings. Despite the fact that they are about the creation of the universe, the Christian creation stories are not trying to give us a literal account of how we were created. Instead, what these stories do is ask us to consider the questions of who and why we are.

Another problem is that when we consider these stories of our beginnings, we tend to want to analyze every little detail. We must remember that the stories are not literally about our creation, but

1 "Catechism of the Catholic Church," paragraph #2357, http://www.vatican.va/archive/ccc_css/archive/catechism/p3s2c2a6.htm (accessed 30 May 2016).

are metaphors meant to convey understandings of the nature of humanity. While metaphor is useful it is never perfect. It is by definition an approximation of something and if we look too closely and assign meaning to every nitty gritty detail, the metaphor will fall apart. Metaphor works best to convey general truths.

Like the stories of creation, the story of the Fall, the story of Adam and Eve ejected from the Garden of Eden because they ate from the Tree of Knowledge against the wishes of the Divine Presence, is not meant to be literal, but is instead, as Paul Tillich asserts, a symbol of the universal human situation.[1] The issue is how we interpret that situation. Traditional theology has often focused on "original sin," an inescapable state of human sinfulness based on the supposed disobedience of Adam and Eve. This turns the Fall into a story of humans as inherently evil, people who cannot help but do wrong.

Understanding humans as inherently evil or bad does not reflect our true nature, however, which is one of love and goodness. It also misunderstands the concept of sin, which I will argue later has nothing to do with being wrong or bad. The first creation story clearly states that the Divine saw what it had created out of itself, out of love, and declared it very good.[2] However we interpret the rest of the story, it tells us quite plainly that all of Creation, including human beings, was created as inherently good. If we make the story of Adam and Eve about sin and the evilness of humanity by focusing on their disobedience, we will be led down the wrong path. Instead, the most important element of this story regarding the human situation is not the disobedience of Adam and Eve but their ejection from the Garden of Eden.

The story of Adam and Eve is partly about identity. It asks fundamental questions about ourselves: Who are we? Why are we? It's a story that searches for meaning and seeks insights into our ultimate identity. The story says that Adam and Eve are created as

1 Tillich, *Systematic Theology, Vol. 2*, (Chicago: The University of Chicago Press, 1975), 29.

2 Genesis 1:31

companions for the Divine Presence, who tells them that if they eat the fruit of the tree of knowledge they will die. But then a serpent tries to undermine their relationship with the Divine, telling them that they are being lied to and that nothing bad will happen. Indeed, the serpent claims if they eat the fruit then they themselves will become like gods. And they choose to eat the fruit and do become in a sense like gods, discovering that they are free to choose. They choose to actualize their freedom and by doing so become fully human, separating themselves from the Divine Presence, which is symbolized in their ejection from the Garden of Eden. In becoming fully human in their identity, they forego their ultimate identity in the Divine Presence. Ironically, our spiritual journey as human beings is to find this unity again, to become reunited with the Divine.

The story of the Fall, then, is not declaring humanity to be inherently bad, but is trying to tell us that the human situation, our nature, is one of separation from the Divine Presence, or what Tillich calls existential estrangement.[1] This separation is not a value judgement against humans. It does not make them bad. Instead, it is a result of the Creation itself. Tillich tells us that this estrangement or separation from the Divine Presence is basic to what it means to be human. To be human is to be individualized selves that have freedom of choice as well as knowledge and self-awareness of the consequences of our choices, and this "means being separated in some way from everything else."[2] If there was no separation, then human freedom could not exist. But since humans are free they have not and cannot exist in any other way than under the conditions of separation from the Divine Presence.[3]

The Fall refers to this separation, which cannot be rectified without divine help. We've fallen and we can't get up. We are separated from the Divine Presence but need the electrifying gravity of Love to guide, or pull, us back to reunion. That is how we are

1 Tillich, *Systematic Theology, Vol. 2*, 44.
2 Tillich, *Systematic Theology, Vol. 1*, 170.
3 Tillich, *Systematic Theology, Vol. 2*, 41.

created and, contrary to what many believe, this does not make us bad or evil. The Divine Presence intended us to live as free creatures and yet freedom is not freedom unless it is exercised. This is how we are intended to be.

The Deathly Hallows: Incarnations of Divinity

However imperfect they may be, these creation stories still provide us with important insights into human nature. When the Divine Presence states that humanity is created in its image, the many people who don't fit the model imposed by the Everyone-must-be-like-me God "are reminded that, in the multiplicity of their racial, sexual, and spiritual identities, they are created in the image and likeness of God."[1] Just as we should reject popular understandings of the Fall as indicating any inherent evilness in humanity, we also need to reject doctrines which use the creation stories to shore up patriarchal power structures or to enforce heterosexual norms and gender dualities. Others have successfully argued against such interpretations of the Fall story and I won't bother to repeat their arguments here.[2] The human as an image of the multiplicity of the Divine Presence affirms the goodness of our being in all of our uniqueness and diversity.

For Mary Daly the feminist movement created new possibilities of relationship with the Divine Presence by "refusing to be objectified and by affirming being."[3] The affirmation of being, of inherent worth, is critical for those such as people of color, women, queer people, and others who have had the shame of non-being emblazoned on their chest like a scarlet letter. The Santa-for-adults God and the Everyone-must-be-like-me God have become tools of society and white patriarchal church systems to make women, queer people, and racial minorities disappear, to make them not

---

1 Cheng, *Rainbow Theology: Bridging Race, Sexuality, and Spirit*, (New York: Seabury Books, 2013), 108. See also Genesis 1:26.

2 For example: Phyllis Trible, *God and the Rhetoric of Sexuality* and Ken Stone, *Practicing Safer Texts*.

3 Daly, 39.

matter. These erroneous conceptions of the Divine are used to try to force people to conform to the approved models of how to look and how to behave. And those who cannot or will not do so are discarded and demonized. They are turned into non-beings, people who no longer matter, who are somehow sub-human. However, the multiplicity of the Divine Presence as infinite incarnation affirms with Daly our being-ness, that we are worthy and that we do matter.

For Tillich, non-being plays an important role in his concept of the Divine Presence. The human lives with the anxiety of their mortality, in fear of the threat of non-being.[1] Certainly, Tillich is correct that humans live in fear of their perceived finitude. This can clearly be seen in our culture's popular obsession with what happens after death. One literary example can be found in J. K. Rowling's Harry Potter fantasy novels where the Elder Wand, the Resurrection Stone and the Cloak of Invisibility form the Deathly Hallows, a set of tools which allows one to master death. Interestingly, the symbol of the Deathly Hallows, a line and a circle enclosed in a triangle, seems very trinitarian, very three-in-one. We might even link the Elder Wand, a symbol of power, to the Divine Presence, the Resurrection Stone to Jesus, and the Cloak of Invisibility to the Holy Spirit and begin to wonder what it might mean to link the Trinity with the idea of mastering death.

As previously mentioned, the Trinity is also a symbol of the Divine Presence's multiplicity, the infinite incarnation of the Divine Presence in Creation, including humanity. What does this trinitarian assertion of multiplicity say about death and human finitude? Might it be telling us that we are ultimately as infinite as the Divine Presence that is incarnated within us? Perhaps we are not truly finite. That is, if human beings are manifestations of the Divine and the Divine is infinite, then it seems reasonable that humans in their true nature transcend the finite, fleshy world of which we are a part.

---

1 Tillich, *Systematic Theology, Vol. 1*, 191.

Scripture alludes to the divine nature of human beings, referring to humanity as the children of the Divine Presence with the implication that we come from the Divine's essence.[1] Indeed, the creation stories found in Genesis assert that we are created in the Divine's image and animated by the Divine's Spirit.[2] Patrick Cheng also affirms the divinity of humans, stating that "human nature was fundamentally transformed in the incarnation and Christ event. God emptied Godself of divinity (that is, kenosis) in the incarnation so that humanity could be filled with divinity."[3] I would argue, however, that the divinity found in humans was not a result of the Christ coming to this world. Such reasoning would seem to denigrate the value of all those who lived before the Christ. The divinity of humans has been true from the beginning of time and was accomplished in the original Creation, the original pouring out of the Divine Presence into the universe. The Christ serves to further reveal this truth to us. As Catherine Keller states, "the grandeur of this incarnate logos [Christ] lies precisely *in its illumination of the word enfleshed in every creature of the creation*."[4]

Reflecting upon humans as incarnations of the divine, there are several analogies we might ponder, none of them perfect. We might think of the original creation as the Divine Presence emptying itself into the universe like one might dump a jigsaw puzzle onto a table. All of the separated pieces, each of importance, each part of the Divine Presence, seek to be reunited into wholeness, into the completed puzzle, the image of which is revealed to us through Jesus the Christ, the great illuminator.

Or, we might imagine a circle where the outer edge of the circle represents the physical world.[5] The infinitesimal center of

1 For example, see Psalm 82:6 / John 10:34, Matthew 5:9, Matthew 5:44-45, John 1:12-12, John 11:51-52, John 12:35-36, Romans 8:14-19, etc.

2 Genesis 1:27 and 2:7

3 Cheng, *From Sin to Amazing Grace*, 57.

4 Keller, *On the Mystery*, 152. The emphasis is mine.

5 This metaphor is inspired by Timothy Freke and Peter Gandy, J*esus and the Lost Goddess: The Secret Teachings of the Original Christians* (New York: Harmony Books, 2001), 63-65.

the circle represents the Divine Presence. We, as incarnations of the divine, are the infinite number of radii connecting the center to the outer edge. As we move our focus toward the center, we move closer to the Divine Presence and to each other. As we move our focus outward, we move farther from the Divine Presence and away from each other. But, we are always connected to both the center and the outer edge. Each being a unique radius, we all connect to a different spot on the physical realm, giving each of us a different perspective, a slightly different view of reality. The Divine Presence interacts with the physical realm through us as the totality of all our different perspectives. This totality of the Divine includes each one of us. For Creation to be whole, we need to all move our focus to the center.

Another metaphorical way to approach this concept of the divinity of humans would be to imagine the Divine Presence as a vast river of love. We are like water from the river taken out and placed in a jug or bottle or any number of wonderfully unique containers. To be one with the Divine is to float in this river, following the ebb and flow of love. The jug may be floating in the river in harmony with the Divine's currents or sometimes it might be snagged on a rock, struggling to find the current. Or it might be sitting on the bank trying to figure out how to return home to the river, yearning for the Divine Presence.

All of these metaphors not only represent our participation in divinity, but also remind us of our separation from it. We are somewhat of a paradox. We are both divinely infinite beings as well as finite fleshy beings. We are not one or the other but both.

Even Tillich with his emphasis on the finitude of humanity seems to see something more in our true nature. He notes the implication in the term estrangement that "one belongs essentially to that from which one is estranged."[1] For Tillich, however, there seems to be a real separation between the Spirit of the Divine Presence, which "is free to work in the spirits" of human beings, and

1 Tillich, *Systematic Theology, Vol. 2*, 45.

those human spirits themselves.[1] But, I wonder, if our true nature essentially belongs to the Divine Presence, whether there is really a difference between Divine Spirit and human spirit. Perhaps our separation from the Divine Presence, the Fall, is not a chasm between two entities, but, in Tillich's words, is a true estrangement, a breaking of something that belongs together and is essentially one. That is, perhaps our continued separation from the Divine Presence, originally a consequence of our freedom, is more of a forgetfulness or unwillingness on the part of human spirit to remember or know what we truly are: that the core of humans, as well as the Divine Presence, is love, one Spirit in infinitely unique and beautiful incarnations.

Of course, in this view of humanity, there is a danger in privileging spirit over body and therefore a supernatural heaven over the world we know. This emphasis on the spirit has often been used to discount the worth of the material world, justifying its abuse as a disposable resource. However, there is an inseparable union between flesh and spirit. We are not just spirit. We are human and that means we are inextricably spirit *and* flesh. To have been incarnated in this world would make no sense if this world didn't matter. And if this world is important, then we must care for it and treasure it. As the mission statement of Phoenix Community Church states, we need to "celebrate the whole person - mind, body, spirit and imagination" and affirm that "the spiritual life cannot be divorced from an active concern for the world."[2]

In light of the Divine Presence's embodiment in all aspects of the universe of matter, Sallie McFague agrees "there can be no spirit/body split: if neither we nor God is disembodied, the denigration of the body, the physical, and matter should end. Such a split makes no sense in our world: spirit and body or matter are on a continuum, for matter is not inanimate substance but throbs of energy, essentially in continuity with spirit."[3] Yet, McFague also

1 Tillich, *The Eternal Now,* (New York: Charles Scribner's Sons, 1963), 87.

2 "Our Mission Statement."

3 McFague, *Models of God*, 74.

affirms, as we might expect if indeed humans are images of the Divine, that spirit, while intimately tied to the body, also transcends the body just as the Divine Presence, while "profoundly immanent in the world," also transcends the world.[1]

Woven Together in Love: Community

All of my attempts to articulate the significance of humans as divine creatures share the implication that the Divine Presence is indeed a multiplicity, in some sense the sum of its many unique and co-constituting parts. Actually, the Divine Presence is much more than the sum of its parts. Like a bright beacon of light made by bringing together a multitude of individual candle flames, the electrifying pull of love that is the Divine Presence is felt most powerfully when we gather together in community. The more people that come together in love, the brighter our light shines and the more strongly the Divine is manifested. The more people that are in prayer together, the more powerful the prayer. The Divine is found within each of us but it is in coming together that we can most powerfully manifest the Divine Presence in our lives. Helping each other on our journeys by nurturing and loving each other, we also nurture and love ourselves and the Divine within because we are all one at our deepest level of being.

The mission statement of Phoenix Community Church provides a wonderful foundation for reflecting upon Christian community. The mission statement is not so much about mission as it is a lovely and eloquent statement of what it means to be in community with each other. It describes what a church community could, and probably should, aspire to be.

Growing Community

The mission statement begins with the assertion that church community is supposed to be about spiritual growth: "Phoenix is a church community that encourages spiritual growth. Questions

1 Ibid., 183.

are taken seriously, and the people of Phoenix share the struggles and joys of being alive." Too often churches get caught up worrying about more quantifiable kinds of growth, worrying about finances and how many people are in worship every Sunday. However, worrying about money or attendance takes our focus away from our relationship with the Divine and each other. It emphasizes worldly measures of success and not necessarily the positive impact of the community. Finances and numbers of people may sometimes be useful tools for reflection, but they should never be the goals of a church. We shouldn't waste our time feeling bad or inadequate about how much money our church has or how many people are in Sunday worship.

Church community is instead about spiritual growth. Perhaps better measurements for our Christian communities are the amount of love and compassion we display in our thoughts, words, and actions. But how does one measure that? It's not easy. It's subtle and subjective. Perhaps all we can do is try to create the conditions for spiritual growth and trust that the Divine Presence will bring new life to bloom in our midst.

Just as we nurture a plant, giving it good soil, water, and the nutrients it needs to grow, we need to care for our spiritual lives, giving them what they need to flourish and grow. Jesus tells the parable of the man who went out sowing seeds.[1] Some seeds fell on a hard path and were not able to take root. Likewise, hard hearts keep us from growing. We need open hearts and minds to foster growth. The Phoenix Community Church mission statement states we need to take questions seriously. Questions open our hearts and minds to the new and mysterious. The willingness to ask tough questions of ourselves and of the world softens our souls so that the seeds of growth might take root.

Jesus' parable goes on to say some seeds fell on rocky soil and the roots weren't able to go deeply enough to survive. To grow we need to work to get the rocks out so that we can sink our roots deeply. What is in our way? What's keeping us from finding a spir-

1 Mark 4:1-9

itual depth that will anchor us and keep us growing through times of trouble? Apathy? Depression? Selfishness? There are so many things that potentially keep us from a deeper trust in and relationship with the Divine. But when we find those rocks we would be well served to pry them out and put them aside. And that may take assistance. We'll need the Divine's help. We'll need the help of each other. We'll need community.

Jesus also says some of the sower's seeds fell into the thorns and were choked. We need good community around us, not thorny people who only want to use us for their own benefit but people who recognize our interdependence and want to help us grow. To grow we need a community of mutually compassionate and supportive people. This is what Paul is talking about in his letter to Ephesians when he writes, "But speaking the truth in love, we must grow up in every way into him who is the head, into Christ, from whom the whole body, joined and knit together by every ligament with which it is equipped, as each part is working properly, promotes the body's growth in building itself up in love."[1]

Paul uses the metaphor of the church as the body of Christ to call for a unity which fosters growth. But this isn't a unity that tries to make everyone the same. The Spirit binds us together with love as one body in Christ but each of us with our own unique gifts. All of those wonderful, unique and precious gifts come together to build up the body, helping it to grow to maturity, helping it to be Divine love in the world as Christ was.

When we have good soil, when we have open hearts and minds, when we work at removing our spiritual rocks, when we surround ourselves with loving community, then the seeds of growth can take root. In his parable, Jesus says that the seeds that found the good soil "brought forth grain, growing up and increasing and yielding thirty and sixty and a hundredfold."[2]

Growth also takes ongoing care. A house plant, for example, even if it has the soil, water, and nutrition it needs can still become

1 Ephesians 4:15-16
2 Mark 4:8

pot-bound. Plants need to have room to continue to grow. If they don't, the roots of the plant become cramped and form a tightly packed mass that inhibits growth. When that happens, they need to be moved to a larger pot so they will remain healthy and keep growing. An otherwise healthy church can become pot-bound, too. It forms walls, whether metaphorical or real, that cause it to form a tightly packed mass and keep it from growing. A pot-bound community thinks "what can visitors do for us" instead of "what can we do for visitors?" Maybe the community has stopped asking questions or comes to suffer a kind of spiritual attention deficit disorder that keeps it from going too deeply into its relationship with the Divine Presence. Church communities can also keep themselves hidden behind the walls of their physical building and away from the world so that only a very few people know they even exist. We can't isolate ourselves from the world and continue to grow spiritually.

It is in struggling with hard questions as a supportive, loving community that we open the door for our spiritual growth as individuals and as communities. We need to ask theological questions, practical questions, and questions about process. We need to ask serious, difficult questions. We are called to growth because if we stop growing, then we've begun dying. We are called to grow spiritually as individuals within community. We are called to always be learning, to always be growing, to always be expecting and reaching out for transformation and new life. Coming together as a questioning, supportive, growing community, we each bring the spark of the Divine that resides within us, sparks that the love and compassion of the Divine Presence can fan into a fire that burns brightly within us so that the whole world may see it and be comforted.

What about challenged?

Celebrating Community

Christian community not only recognizes our human differences but rejoices and celebrates those differences. The Phoenix Community Church mission statement declares that

> ... the people of Phoenix share the struggles and joys of being alive.
>
> All are welcomed at Phoenix, regardless of age, abilities, sex, race, sexual orientation, gender identity and expression. We wish to rejoice in our differences while we affirm our similarities.
>
> At Phoenix, we encourage and celebrate the whole person - mind, body, spirit and imagination. We use new forms of worship that speak to a church community with a variety of beliefs. We attempt to avoid language that is hurtful or exclusive.[1]

Just as Christian community should be a spiritually growing community, it should also be a celebrating community. We are on this journey together as one body. We need to remember our unity but we also need to remember to celebrate our differences. One of the ways we can do this is worshipping in ways that speak to all aspects of our selves and the diversity of our gifts and beliefs. For example, the use of inclusive language, which seeks to counteract the traditional privileging of the male over the female, can also honor our differences by using language that includes and celebrates all people.

In his letter to the Corinthians, the apostle Paul asks us to imagine a body where the foot doesn't think it's important because it's not a hand.[2] Or the ear doesn't want to be part of the body because it can't be an eye. This vision of various body parts arguing with each other, being petty and jealous of each other, is absurd. And that's the point. It's absurd to think parts of a body could go off alone, ignoring the importance and necessity of the body's functioning as a whole. This analogy for the Body of Christ is meant to stress that human beings are communal creatures. We need each other and are dependent on each other. Our desire for

---

1 "Our Mission Statement."

2 1 Corinthians 12:12-27

community is part of the Divine's design. It is, I think, one of the ways in which we are made in the image of the Divine Presence. And yet it is equally absurd to think that to come together as a body means we all have to be the same with the same ideas and same gifts. The foot can't be the hand and the ears can't be the eyes. But they are all important to the body. They are all reasons for celebration.

This talk of the body doesn't apply just to Christians. The body of Christ is also the body of all Creation. It includes every last person, every last animal, and every last plant or rock or grain of sand. Every last bit of Creation is precious and cause for celebration. When we lose any of it we are all diminished. When any of it is harmed we are all harmed. We humans tend to forget this too often. Instead of celebrating our differences we try to dismember the body. We see people who seem different and we want to separate ourselves like the foot from the hand. It's absurd. Or we abuse the land, cutting down forests, strip mining, fracking, dumping oil into our rivers. That too is absurd.

We need to remember our unity. We need to celebrate our differences and stand up when we see injustice. When we encounter racism we need to assert that black lives matter because somehow our society wants to try to deny that. When our government lets corporations abuse sacred land for a fast buck we need to stand up and say "stop!" This is part of what it means to be a celebrating community because if we truly celebrate and rejoice in how each person and each part of creation enriches our joint lives with their uniqueness, then we won't want to lose even the smallest part of this body of Christ.

The Phoenix Community Church mission statement and the apostle Paul both ask Christian community to rejoice and celebrate in our unique gifts. We are not all alike. We all have things we can do well and other things that we don't do so well. We don't all have the same beliefs or opinions. We don't always agree, but it is together that we make a whole body. Each of us in that body is loved and important. Each of us is an image of the Holy. The Phoenix Community Church mission statement also reminds us to not only celebrate the differences in each other but to celebrate that we as individuals are also complex creations, with many different aspects that come together to make us whole.

We need to celebrate those parts too: our mind, body, spirit, and imagination. Sometimes we forget the many parts of ourselves as individuals. We might favor the mind and forget the body. Or we might worry only about the body and forget the spirit. The Phoenix Community Church mission statement invites us to remember to seek our own personal wholeness, that each aspect of ourselves is also important, loved, and precious to the Divine Presence. We are called to be who the Divine created us to be, loving ourselves — mind, body, spirit, and imagination — just as we are loved by the Divine Presence. No one ever needs to compare themselves to anyone else.

As Paul says, we are all part of the body of Christ. When one member suffers, all suffer. When one member is honored, all share the joy. To celebrate our differences is also to care for each other with love and compassion. Each one of us is an important part of that body, bringing our own Divine-given uniqueness to form an amazing and wonderful whole. Let us never forget to rejoice and celebrate in our differences. Let us be a celebrating community.

Supporting Community

The mission statement of Phoenix Community Church also calls Christian community to be mutually supportive: "The people of Phoenix share good times together and try to support one another during hard times." At his last supper with the disciples, as recorded in the gospel of John, Jesus gives us an example of service to those around him by washing the feet of his disciples and telling the disciples to do likewise, reinforcing this with the command that they love one another, asserting that by their love will they be known.[1] This command is about a new way of relating to those around us that goes against the grain of the rugged indi-

1 John 13:1-35

vidualism which is idolized in American culture. This new way of life is grounded in Jesus' relationship with the disciples and with the Divine Presence and is shaped by the example he sets for us: teaching, healing, and serving all of the Divine's beloved children with humility. It's about bearing one another's burdens.[1] It's about living as a supporting community.

To love someone in the sense that Jesus is talking about is not necessarily to like them or be their best friend. It's not an emotional reaction to someone, either. Instead, loving someone as Jesus commands us to do means realizing and always remembering that they are a beloved child of the Divine Presence and that they are worthy of that love. This kind of love is an active love, a compassionate love, and a being-with love. It means to rejoice with each other in times of good fortune and to support each other in our times of difficulty. It means being servants to one another. To love one another is perhaps more about doing than it is about feeling.

We are bound together in our common experience of humanity, but it is in the Holy essence that resides within each one of us that we are connected. It is because of the Divine within that we know that we are each loved and that we are each worthy of love. If we are true followers of the way of the Divine Presence, Jesus tells us, then we will be known by our love for each other, for all humanity, and for Creation itself because we will recognize, respect, and have compassion for the Divine within all things.

Sometimes we forget. Maybe we feel sorry for ourselves and ignore or even lash out at others instead of loving them. Maybe we forget to look for the Christ in the other, forgetting that they are a worthy, beloved child of the Divine Presence. Sometimes we need to stop and take a deep breath, look around us, and remind ourselves of the Divine goodness within each of us. Even if that other person is the most difficult person we know, that Divine spark is within them too, perhaps just waiting to be fanned into a flame by the winds of our love.

---

1 Galatians 6:2

We shouldn't forget our own worthiness either. The claim that everyone is worthy of love isn't just about everyone else. It applies to us, too. It can be difficult to accept the support that we need. We need to not only support and be a servant to those around us, to love one another as Jesus commanded, but to also open our own hearts and lives and to accept the support and love offered to us. By opening up to those around us who are trying to help, we open ourselves to the Presence of the Divine, for we are the Divine's voice and hands for each other.

Christian community is growing community, celebrating community, and supporting community. In community, in meaningful relationship with each other and with the Divine Presence, we find abundant life. As the Phoenix Community Church mission statement says, "We do not want to become self-satisfied and complacent, but seek instead to be a life-giving church community that reaches out and welcomes in." Instead of self-satisfied, we want to always be growing. Instead of complacent, we don't want to take anything for granted but be grateful and celebrate all that we have.

To be a supportive community is also to be a life-giving community. In their book "Leading Causes of Life" Gary Gunderson and Lawrence Pray suggest that our focus shouldn't be on preventing death but nurturing life.[1] They name what they understand to be the five leading causes of life: connection, coherence, agency, blessing, and hope. All five of these causes are found in a supporting community, in the act of reaching out and welcoming in. Supporting each other:

- fosters connections and relationships
- creates coherence, or a sense of belonging
- requires agency, asking us to step out and risk ourselves in doing for others
- makes visible the blessings of our lives together
- and brings hope and the assurance that with each other and the Divine Presence, all will be well.

1 Gunderson and Pray, *Leading Causes of Life: Five Fundamentals to Change the Way You Live Your Life*, (Nashville, TN: Abingdon Press, 2009).

A supporting community creates the conditions for abundant life to flourish. When we love one another, when we support each other, when we rejoice together in our blessings, when we share our burdens, easing our load with love and compassion, we find ourselves in the presence of the Holy. We find abundant life.

Resurrecting Community

Melanie Morrison, one of the founding pastors of Phoenix Community Church, has explained the significance of the church's chosen name:

> The phoenix is a mythological bird that rises out of its own ashes to new life. This Egyptian myth was appropriated by the early Christian church as a symbol of resurrection. The people in Kalamazoo who gathered to form a new church also appropriated this myth as a symbol of our belief that resurrection is possible out of the ashes of discrimination, self-hatred, and oppression.[1]

The idea of resurrection, that new life can spring from death, the affirmation that from the midst of our darkest times the growth of something new will appear, is central to what Christian community is. It is central to the hope that we find in Christ. To be clear, I'm not talking about resurrection as life after physical death, although that promise brings a different kind of hope, but instead I'm referring to the new life we find in Christ in this world in the here and now. The trust we place in the assurance of resurrection, also appears in the last two paragraphs of the Phoenix Community Church mission statement:

> We believe that the spiritual life cannot be divorced from an active concern for the world. Individually and collectively, we seek to challenge oppression and injustice, and work for peace and the preservation of the environment.

1 Morrison.

> To fulfill our mission, we need the presence of the spirit and the support of one another. We seek to forgive ourselves and each other when we fail, and to accept the responsibility to begin anew.[1]

The last sentence is perhaps the most important, most profound, and most difficult aspiration we can have for church community. This is resurrection we're talking about. When we have disagreements, when life becomes overwhelming, when we have to deal with illness and financial concerns and we don't know what to do, when it feels like we're failing, this is when we have to seek to forgive both ourselves and each other, put our trust in the Divine Presence, and begin anew. Paul, in his letters to the Christians in Rome, assures us that as followers of Christ we are united with Christ in his death and resurrection.[2] As Christ died and was resurrected, so too we die to our old selves and are resurrected into new beings that we might live a new life, a life that we couldn't have imagined before.

In his letter to the Ephesians, Paul expands on this idea of a new life.[3] He says our old lives, our lives outside of the Divine Presence, are corrupted by following illusory desires. We put other gods such as pleasure, power, and wealth ahead of the loving Divine Presence. These things may not be inherently bad, but they become idols, illusory desires, when they become the foundation of how we live our lives. When we pursue happiness by pursuing pleasure, power, or wealth, it's like grasping at straws.

What's real, what we can truly hold onto, is the love offered to us by the Divine Presence. The true joy of life is found in the Divine, when we overthrow the little gods in our lives in a spiritual revolution so that we can find our true selves as part of the body of Christ in a life lived in love. This new life is one where the Divine Presence which is the electrifying gravity of love becomes our

1 "Our Mission Statement."

2 Romans 6:4-5

3 Ephesians 4:22-32

foundation. In this life there is honesty instead of lies. Anger doesn't rule our lives. We share instead of steal. We seek to build others up instead of tear them down. It is a life of kindness, compassion, and forgiveness.

New life in Christ is about an entirely new attitude toward life. This is a resurrection life, a life not of despair but of hope and new beginnings where we recognize not only our need for the presence of the Divine but our need for each other and our need for growing, celebrating, and supporting community. To paraphrase John F. Kennedy, it's a life that calls us to ask not what our neighbor can do for us but what we can do for our neighbor.

To be the resurrected and resurrecting people that the Divine Presence calls us to be, we need both the Divine and each other. We need to nurture life-giving relationships. Being a resurrecting community isn't just about personally experiencing new life in Christ, but it's also about creating new life in the world around us — and I don't mean evangelism. This sentiment is reflected in the creation stories when the Divine Presence gives humanity "dominion" over creation and when the first human is placed in the Garden of Eden to "till it and keep it."[1]

Sallie McFague believes that caring for the earth "is our primary vocation as God's partners in helping creation to flourish."[2] As care-takers of the world, of humans and human culture as well as animals and natural resources, we enter into a relationship with that world. McFague states that "God's household is the *whole* planet: it is composed of human beings living in interdependent relations with all other life-forms and earth processes."[3] Likewise, for Catherine Keller, this is a very deep connection: "we do not exist outside of our relationships. We become who we are in relationship: we are network creatures."[4]

1 Genesis 1:26 and Genesis 2:15
2 McFague, *A New Climate*, 34.
3 Ibid., 33.
4 Keller, *On the Mystery*, 32.

The difficult work of resurrection takes trust in the Divine Presence and it takes the support of one another. The Phoenix Community Church mission statement calls it a responsibility. As followers of the Divine Presence's way, we not only have the promise of new beginnings when life gets rough, but we have the responsibility to begin anew. It's difficult work because sometimes we will fail to trust the Divine Presence and to support each other. We'll fail both as individuals and as community to take up that responsibility to actively seek a new way.

When we fail we are called to forgive ourselves and each other, put our trust in the Divine, and begin anew. It's a never ending process. Resurrection is not a one-time thing. It is a continual process. We are always in the middle of our next resurrection. We are always in the middle of beginning anew. A new, resurrected life may not look like the old life at all. When we forgive and begin anew, our lives might be different, with different people, and with a different purpose. But we are called to trust that resurrection is possible out of the ashes of our failures and the world's failures.

Sometimes we don't necessarily fail but maybe we flounder around for awhile not knowing what we're doing or where we're going. These too are times that every community goes through — and these too are times to stop, forgive, trust the leading of the Divine Presence, and begin anew. But that new life might be different. New life that is the same is not new life. New life means change and transformation. It means asking what needs to change. It means asking what dream the Divine wants us to dream now.

The continual process of renewal and rejuvenation that is a resurrection life can be difficult. Trading in the comfort of "what is" for the hope and challenge of "what can be" is not for the feint-hearted. Christian community, however, is called to be a resurrected and resurrecting community. Even when life threatens to overwhelm us, the Divine Presence promises us new life through Christ.

As images of the Divine, humans are intended to be in community — growing, celebrating, supporting, and resurrecting community. It is part of our essential nature. Relationship and community are profoundly reflected in the creation stories when the Divine Presence states it is creating humanity "in our image, according to our likeness,"[1] which immediately brings to mind the Divine Presence as the Trinity, as the interdependent relationships of co-creating and co-forming multiplicity.

The metaphor of people woven together in community is an important one for Phoenix Community Church. One of the church's favorite songs uses the metaphors of images in a tapestry and instruments in a symphony to talk about diversity and community. In sentiments similar to my own proposal of each of us as incarnations of love, the song states, "Now the Christ in me greets the Christ in thee, in one great family" and the chorus ends:

> Weave, weave, weave us together.
> Weave us together in unity and love.
> Weave, weave, weave us together.
> Weave us together, together in love.[2]

Of course, Christian community is not just community with other humans. Community includes all of Creation and the Divine Presence itself. In our separation from ourselves, from Creation, and from the Divine, we find ourselves yearning for this community, for reunion. To bridge the gap of this separation, we need the Divine Presence, the electrifying energy of love, that pulls us toward that wholeness, that reunion with love, with the Divine Presence itself.

---

1 Genesis 1:26

2 "Weave," Copyright (c) 1979 Rosemary Crow.

Chapter 4 Discussion Questions

1. Do you understand humans as either inherently good or inherently evil? Why?
2. How do we favor either our spiritual or physical aspects over the other?
3. What can you do to develop relationship with the Divine within you?
4. Where do you find community in your life? What are the characteristics of a healthy spiritual community?

5 Separated but Together

Thoughts on Sin and Suffering

Neither Naughty nor Nice: Defining Sin

Used to bolster the power and influence of the institutional church, the concept of sin may be one of the most abused Christian doctrines. A cynical view of the doctrine of sin might perceive how the institutional church historically has sought to establish our human sinfulness, convincing us that we are inherently bad or even evil, while lowering self-esteem and inducing guilt, not necessarily over anything we've done but because of our very existence. Jesus is proclaimed as our salvation, but that often seems to be little more than a smokescreen because approved access to Jesus is through the church. The church itself becomes the only path to forgiveness and salvation, with the threat of eternal damnation looming over our heads as the alternative. One might come to understand such a doctrine to be primarily a vehicle to keep people under the power of the institutional church.

The popular understanding of sin as wrong-doing, especially when combined with the idea of original sin, has done much harm. People are beat down and ostracized over their "sins." Inherent sin was once used to justify the slavery of blacks.[1] Even today, the perception of black people as somehow bad and therefore inferior is integral to sustaining racism in our culture. Queer people have also suffered from the stigma of their so-called sinfulness. Theologian Patrick Cheng notes that "sin-talk remains at the heart of the oppression and suffering — emotional, spiritual, psychological, and

---

1 Felicia R. Lee, "From Noah's Curse to Slavery's Rationale," *The New York Times*, 1 November, 2003, http://www.nytimes.com/2003/11/01/arts/from-noah-s-curse-to-slavery-s-rationale.html (accessed 8 January, 2016).

physical — that LGBT people experience today."[1] Sin understood as inherent wrong-doing and badness leads to the condemnation of queer people as evil at the very core of who they are.

It is no wonder that one tendency, especially among queer people, is to reject talk of sin altogether because such talk has been used to reject them. Yet, the idea of sin is deeply embedded in Christianity. At its best, it can help us reflect on our nature and the ethical conundrum of how we label things as good and bad. It can remind us that we fall short of perfection and that we need the help of the Divine Presence and the help of family, friends, and spiritual community to make it through this life. The idea of sin can also remind us of the importance of forgiveness.

What is needed is a way of understanding what sin really means. Thinking of sin strictly as wrong-doing is fraught with too many problems to be useful any longer. The answer, in fact, lies within Christian tradition. While the concept may be new to many church-going Christians, Catherine Keller notes that sin was traditionally defined as "separation from God"[2] and Paul Tillich, rejecting sin as a "failure to act in the right way,"[3] defines it as a "state of estrangement from that to which one belongs — God, one's self, one's world."[4] Therefore, sin as a concept means to be separated from the Divine Presence, and thus from Divine love, by which I don't mean the warm fuzzy feelings we sometimes associate with love, but instead a deep caring and compassion for Creation, for other people, and for ourselves. If we talk of sin as an action it refers to those things we might do or think that cause us to be separated from the Divine Presence, those things that keep us from being caring and compassionate, that keep us from being loved or loving others, that sabotage our relationships with the Divine Presence and each other. At times in our lives and to varying degrees, we all find ourselves separated from the Divine Presence. It

1 Cheng, *From Sin to Amazing Grace*, 6.
2 Keller, *On the Mystery*, 79.
3 Tillich, *Eternal Now*, 51.
4 Tillich, *Systematic Theology, Vol. 2*, 46.

is part of being human. In fact, as discussed previously, separation is a consequence of realizing our freedom as humans. In this sense, original sin does exist — every human being experiences this separation and the corresponding yearning for reunion.

Of course, the term sin is so tied to the idea of wrong-doing it is tempting to reject it completely and seek other ways of expressing what sin represents. However, Tillich argues that the word sin shouldn't be replaced because it implies a personal responsibility that is lacking in other possible terminology such as separated or his own favored word, estrangement.[1] To talk of our being separated from the Divine says nothing about how that existential gap is to be bridged. The term sin carries with it the implication of our own responsibility for our separation or, perhaps more accurately, for our reunion. The Divine Presence invites and pulls us toward reunion, but in our freedom we must choose to follow.

If we are not to reject the terminology of sin, we must be clear about what it does and doesn't mean. Defining "sin" as a description of the human state of separation from the Divine Presence, as reflected in the Fall, and "sins" as those acts which reinforce and further that separation, which turn us away from the Divine Presence, leads to a couple of helpful implications and corrections to the popular definition of sin as wrong-doing.

First, sin as separation is contextual. What is sin for one person may or may not be sin for another person as it depends entirely on whether it widens or narrows their personal separation from the Divine. For example, one might consider those who drink alcohol. For some it is an addiction which keeps them from living into their potential in life, negatively affecting those around them, and is therefore a sin, widening their separation from the Divine Presence which is love. For others, drinking alcohol is not a sin but simply a pleasure which is mostly neutral to their life and those around them. For some, one might argue it actually increases their enjoyment of life and therefore brings them even closer to the Divine Presence. This makes moral judgments very tricky as they become

1 Ibid.

complex and highly contextual. Of course, there are also acts, such as murder, which can be more generally understood as sinful because the negative ways in which they affect the relationship with the Divine for both perpetrator and victim are more obvious and more consistent.

The contextual ambiguity of sin is also implicit in Sallie McFague's description of sin as "being conscious of a better way but not choosing it"[1] and Catherine Keller's description of sin as a "blockage" or "obstruction."[2] In McFague's approach, the ambiguity is apparent in the problem of knowing what the better way is. Any human being knows from personal experience that this is not always a simple task. In Keller's description of sin, the ambiguity can be seen in the observation that, since humans are unique and complex individuals, what blocks one from their connection to the Divine may be different for another.

For queer people, this contextual understanding of sin as separation from the Divine Presence turns the widely used criticism of non-heterosexuality as sinful upside down. If queer people were created by the Divine Presence as queer, which is my personal conviction, then it is not being queer that is sinful, but it is remaining in the closet, denying one's queerness, that is sinful.[3] When it comes to our sexuality, whatever it may be, the Divine Presence has made each of us uniquely the way we are. To embrace our sexuality is not sinning, but quite the opposite. To embrace our sexuality is to embrace ourselves as beloved creations of the Holy. To sin would be to deny our sexuality, to reject what the Divine Presence has made, because to do so would further estrange us from the Divine. The popular concept of sin as wrong-doing actually leads queer people further into a state of sin when it convinces them to attempt to deny and change their Divinely given nature.

1 McFague, *A New Climate*, 153.

2 Catherine Keller, *Face of the Deep: A Theology of Becoming* (London and New York: Routledge, 2003), 214.

3 In *From Sin to Amazing Grace*, Cheng proposes seven "deadly sins" based on models of the "Queer Christ." The closet and conformity are two of these.

Second, sin as separation is not a value judgment. Although I have already noted the problems of making universal moral judgments in a contextual definition of sin, talking of sin and moral judgments together makes some sense since individual acts can be sinful, separating us or others from the Divine Presence, and thus perhaps called immoral. However, unlike what those who adhere to the concept of the Santa-for-adults God might try to tell us, sin as a state of separation carries no value judgment. Unlike the Santa-for-adults God, the Divine Presence isn't keeping a tally of our sins to determine whether we get a gift or a lump of coal, heaven or hell. Sin does not make us naughty and the appearance of a lack of sin, which is an illusion, does not make us nice. Sin is simply a description of what is. Stating that one is a sinner or living in a state of sin, a state of separation from the Divine Presence, has no implications that one is inherently bad or evil as all people are equally sinful, equally separated from the Divine Presence. The difference is whether we walk toward or away from the Divine.

Just as humans can resist gravity by rocketing themselves into outer space, humans can also resist the pull of Love which is the Divine Presence, separating us from that Love. Sin is in fact a consequence of human freedom.[1] In order to have freedom of action, humans must be separated from the Divine Presence. If there were no separation, then humans would always act as the Divine Presence and would thus have no freedom. The freedom to choose our path in life is a great gift from the Divine Presence who created us. We are not meant to be automatons that unthinkingly live out a preprogrammed existence, but we were created with the flexibility to learn, grow and mature. I believe this is one of the ways in which humanity can be understood to be an image of the Divine. When Adam and Eve ate the forbidden fruit in the Garden of Eden, the serpent was right in a sense.[2] They did become like gods because they actualized their freedom to choose their own path, even if it contradicted the Divine Presence's desires for them. The one thing

1 Tillich, *Systematic Theology, Vol. 2*, 61.

2 Genesis 3:4-5

we cannot choose is whether or not we have freedom. It is the way we were created, the way we are meant to be, and separation from the Divine, or sin, is a necessary consequence.

However, having freedom does not make us bad. While we might label as bad, or bad for us, those things and acts which help maintain or reinforce our separation from the Divine Presence, recognizing sin in our lives is not about naming things we do wrong or making us feel bad or guilty. It is about perceiving the roadblocks and bonds that are keeping us from full relationship with the Divine Presence, keeping us from wholeness.

The Devil is in the Details: Manifestations of Sin

As creatures which are part of the Divine and of which the Divine is part, the human journey is one of seeking reunion with the Divine Presence. It is a journey of following the electrifying pull of love that seeks to bring us to wholeness. To find that wholeness and reunion, we need to learn to use our freedom responsibly, to choose to follow the pull of love instead of choosing other masters such as the temptations of wealth-gathering or the accumulation of power.

If it seems unreasonable to both affirm that humans themselves are divine and separated from the Divine, one might consider again the analogy of a jig-saw puzzle. While the puzzle is pulled apart, with all of the individual pieces separated from itself, it is still a puzzle and each of the pieces are still part of the puzzle with a goal of being reunited as one. Likewise, humans, although incarnations of the Divine, are also separated from the Divine, striving to return to union and to wholeness.

To successfully navigate the journey to wholeness, we also must be aware of how sin manifests in our lives. This is the purpose of the Christian rite of confession. Although confession may have been used by the church in the past to induce guilt and low self-esteem in its followers in order to maintain control of them, such practices should be condemned. Confession actually has an important spiritual role to play. It is an invitation to turn to the Divine Presence and name the ways we act and think which are not in our best interest, which do harm to ourselves and others, and which bind us and hold us back. By confessing our bonds and failings, we bring them into conscious awareness and open ourselves to the transforming work and will of the Divine Presence as it pulls us toward loving wholeness. Confession should never make us feel bad or guilty but instead it should liberate us from our guilt that we might make amends and draw closer to the Divine.

When we think of sin, we typically think of sin as some kind of action against the Divine Presence that compounds our own personal separateness from the Divine. Sin can be that, but it would be dangerously misleading to think sin is only that. As the saying goes, the devil is in the details. If we understand the concept of sin to only apply between individuals and a transcendent, heavenly Divine Presence, we will miss other, perhaps even more insidious, manifestations of sin in our lives.

The concept of sin is not meant to shame us but is really meant to remind us that we need to constantly nurture our relationship with the Divine — and not only the transcendent Divine Presence that we might imagine to be far off in heaven, and not only the Divine that resides deep within our own selves, but also the Divine that is encountered in the other, in each of the people we meet every day whether friend or stranger, loved one or enemy. To be estranged from each other is also sin because the Divine Presence is in each of us.

Just as we might say we can sin against the Divine Presence, or act out in ways that reinforce our separation from the Divine, we can also sin against each other or even against Creation. Separation from other human beings or from the Divine Presence's sacred Creation is also damaging to our wholeness. Because of the Divine spark that resides in every human being, to separate ourselves from each other is to also separate ourselves from the Divine. This is why Jesus makes it clear that loving our neighbor is a fundamental principle of how we should live our lives.[1]

How we treat each other is important. When we fail to treat each other with compassion and respect and fail to try to understand each other, we are driving a wedge between us. This too is sin. When we fail to care about the homeless, the poor, the immigrant, and the refugee, we estrange ourselves from our neighbors, our fellow human beings, and thus from the Divine Presence. Too many Christians fail to realize this when they support policies, for example, that make it illegal to feed the homeless in a public park or that seek to deny the basic necessities of life to the poor by keeping wages low so that the wealthy can increase their profits. When, out of our fear, we demonize the immigrant or the refugee because they are not like us and deny them our love, compassion, and active assistance, we create sin in our lives.

Likewise, to abuse the Divine Presence's good Creation is sin. The Divine has breathed its essence not only into human beings, but into all that exists. When we destroy the earth and its resources through actions such as strip mining and fracking and when we denigrate the lives of animals through abusive livestock practices, we destroy and devalue holy creations and thereby separate ourselves from the Divine Presence. We create sin in our lives, both as individuals and as a society.

Sometimes sin is also talked about as a force, even a cosmic force, in the universe. The Apostle Paul does this in his letter to the Romans.[2] For me, sin as a cosmic force doesn't mean the Devil or any kind of evil supernatural being, but instead it represents all the systemic ways that we have built processes and messages into our culture that keep us separated from the Divine and each other. This might also be considered a kind of communal sin, a way in which

---

1 Matthew 22:37-40, Mark 12:28-31, and Luke 10:25-27. Note that the Apostle Paul concurs on the vital importance of this commandment in Romans 13:8-10 and Galatians 5:14.

2 Romans 6:12-14

we as a group culturally, and perhaps unconsciously, contrive to keep ourselves separated from the Divine Presence.

For example, we're taught that wealth is what makes us successful. If we're not rich we're nobody. How important we are depends on how much we own and how much we can claim is ours and ours alone. Our culture repeatedly reinforces this message. We can see it in laws that take resources from the poor and give them to the rich. We can see it in a judicial system that too often slaps rich people on the wrist and sentences poor people and minorities to lengthy prison terms. And we can see it in the mundane, too, such as the advertising that bombards our senses every day and all day, trying to convince us to take what little we do have and spend it on the latest luxury item we don't really need or even want.

These messages that we receive about wealth and power, as well as cultural messages and structures that reinforce racism, sexism, homophobia, and a multitude of other systemic problems, are an example of what I believe Paul means when he talks of the forces of sin. And they are sin. They act to build up our selfish egos and to keep us separated. They work against the Divine's intention that we love each other, that we care for and live with compassion for each other, for Creation and for the Divine Presence.

Sin, all the ways in which we reject and separate ourselves from the Divine, is complex and we sell ourselves short if we simplify it to only mean wrongdoing as defined by the church or those in power. We must pay attention to the detail and complexities of our personal actions but also how we've communally and systematically built up destructive and even malevolent barriers between each other, Creation and the Divine Presence. Only by doing so will we be able to begin to dismantle these barriers and find wholeness and reunion with the Divine.

+ but also as strategy to control resources - see next pgs.

Threat of Apocalypse: Searching for a Christian Response to War

One particularly horrific communal sin is our propensity for war and violence. We live in a time of war. Conflicts exist throughout the world. From our earliest history humanity seems prone to turn to violence in response to our fears. Many people wish to declare the American culture as Christian and at the same time promote war and other forms of violence as the solution to our problems. Yet, to commit violence upon another person or another nation is clearly an egregious sin. We cannot seek to destroy and oppress one another and at the same time pretend we are moving closer to the Divine Presence who commands us to love one another. War and violence clearly separate us from each other and thus from the Divine Presence.

So, then, as Christians, how are we to respond to war? Can we support war under any circumstances? If so, then when is it permissible? Are we called to be pacifists, even if we fear the consequences of such a position?

As a Christian, we may want to turn to the New Testament for guidance, but if we do, the help we find may be minimal. While Jesus' teachings and actions can be read as an anti-imperial political statement,[1] his greatest commandment is one of love and he nowhere advocates violence. However, Catherine Keller contends that the notion of apocalypse and Biblical citations of apocalypse can be found at the root of many human projects, many of them clearly violent and war-like.[2]

When discussing the New Testament's apocalyptic teachings and its views of violence and war, one may also note Jesus' own use of violence in driving the money changers from the temple,[3] as well as noting that, at least part of the time, the disciples traveled

1 Marcus J. Borg and John Dominic Crossan, *The Last Week: What the Gospels Really Teach About Jesus' Final Days in Jerusalem* (San Francisco: HarperCollins, 2007) makes this case convincingly.

2 Keller, *God and Power*, 81.

3 Mark 11:15

armed.[1] When Jesus does seem to speak of violence, such as when telling us to "turn the other cheek,"[2] he seems to not be concerned with violence at the level of war but with inter-personal relationships. I fear that, as with many issues, the Bible will give us no absolutely clear answer to the question of war. What we get is a mixed message and that is with leaving alone the frequently pro-war stance of the Hebrew Bible (or Old Testament, as we sometimes call it). If the Bible doesn't give us definitive answers, do today's modern theologians and political scientists have an answer for war that can help guide Christians?

Many agree that war is a major problem of our time. Theologian Jürgen Moltmann states his belief that "peace is a major theological problem of politics in this decade"[3] and "we are destroying the third world more and more with our armaments race; the two developments are intertwined."[4] Cornel West names war, or "aggressive militarism", as one of the three dogmas, along with "market fundamentalism" and "escalating authoritarianism," that are "leading to the imperial devouring of democracy."[5] Michael Hardt and Antonio Negri state "War is becoming a general phenomenon, global and interminable."[6] For them, war has become so pervasive that "we can no longer imagine or even hope for a real peace."[7]

War is no longer under the control of politics, but has become the "primary organizing principle of society,"[8] with politics as one of the tools of war. War has become the way in which the modern

1 John 18:10

2 Matthew 5:38-39

3 Jürgen Moltmann, "Following Jesus Christ in an Age of Nuclear War" in *The Politics of Discipleship and Discipleship in Politics*, ed. Willard M. Swartley, 49-69 (Eugene, OR: Wipf & Stock Publishers, 2006), 49.

4 Ibid., 51.

5 Cornel West, *Democracy Matters: Winning the Fight Against Imperialism* (New York: Penguin Books, 2004), 146.

6 Michael Hardt and Antonio Negri, *Multitude: War and Democracy in the Age of Empire* (New York: Penguin Books, 2004), 3.

7 Ibid., 5.

8 Ibid., 12.

world is in relationship.[1] War not only serves to destroy what we do not want, but it attempts to build up what we desire in place of the annihilated.[2]

Significantly, Hardt and Negri point out that "a war to create and maintain social order can have no end. It must involve the continuous, uninterrupted exercise of power and violence. In other words, one cannot win such a war, or, rather, it has to be won again every day. War thus becomes virtually indistinguishable from police activity."[3] This is exactly the type of war the U.S. has recently fought in Iraq and Afghanistan: an unending war of social control. The old has been destroyed and the new must be built in our own image. But, war then becomes *police activity*. War becomes the basis for maintaining peace and order, which is quite a paradox since how can war be peace and order when it is by its very definition violence and death?

These wars are also, as we know, not fought just in foreign lands. Hardt and Negri point out the difference between defense and security: "Whereas 'defense' involves a protective barrier against external threats, 'security' justifies a constant martial activity equally in the homeland and abroad."[4] If we want to provide security we must not only employ what West calls the democracy destroying dogma of aggressive militarism, but we must also implement the democracy destroying dogma of escalating authoritarianism here at home in the form of reduced rights and increased domestic governmental espionage.

How do we react to a philosophy of war that has moved from war as a last resort self-defense to war that has even moved past imperialist goals to being used as a pervasive, ongoing tool of reshaping the reality of our world in our own image? As Christians, how can we justify the carnage of war for these purposes, or for any purpose? Indeed, is war even permissible for self-defense?

1 Ibid., 13.
2 Ibid., 20.
3 Ibid., 14.
4 Ibid., 21.

One problem with modern warfare actually lies in the philosophies that try to conduct war while minimizing the losses of human life. Modern technologies of destruction seek to minimize the deaths of soldiers, at least the soldiers of the armies of the world-shapers (i.e. the United States). However, Hardt and Negri assert that "without the horror of war there is less incentive to put an end to it, and war without end … is the ultimate barbarity."[1] While the soldiers of the U.S. incur relatively fewer casualties than past wars, the soldiers and non-combatants of those parts of the world that we are "democratizing" continue to die in disturbing numbers. "Since only one side lacks an incentive to put an end to war," Hardt and Negri go on to ask, "what incentive does a power have to put an end to war if it never suffers from it?"[2] Have we lost an understanding of the evil of war to the point that it has become tolerable as an ongoing part of our lives, with no end in sight?

According to Keller, "Christians have two strong traditions of response to war: the pacifism of the early Christian community, in which John's apocalypse formed, and the just war doctrine, which evolved as an ideal of constraint for the subsequent Christian empires. Both are problematic: pacifism tends to settle for an unjust peace, but a just peace is as difficult to achieve as a just war."[3] As Keller notes, both of these traditional options, pacifism and just war, have their own set of problems. However, it is worth looking briefly at each to see if some kind of answer indeed lies there.

Jürgen Moltmann, noting that the idea of just war "was not developed for the justification of war but for the limitation of war,"[4] lists "the decisive elements of the doctrine of the 'just war':"

3. War must be declared by a legitimate authority; it must serve the common good of the state.
4. It must be conducted with a good intention.

1 Ibid., 46.
2 Ibid.
3 Keller, *God and Power*, 5.
4 Moltmann, "Following Jesus," 57.

5. It must be conducted with the expectation of a good outcome: the general situation after the war must be better than the situation before it.
6. All peaceful means for a resolution of the conflict must have been exhausted.
7. The means of the war may not be worse than the evil which is supposed to be overcome by it, that is, the means must stand in the right relationship to the end.
8. There must be a distinction between soldiers and citizens. The civil population must be protected.[1]

However, if we look closely at these conditions, it is clear that they do not amount to anything in reality because they are dependent on the subjective evaluation of the conquering power. For condition one, we have the question of what constitutes a legitimate authority as well as what it means to "serve the common good." But, regardless, one cannot imagine any war in which any party deciding to enter a war does not consider themselves legitimate or does not see the effort as serving their own interests.

Likewise, condition two seems to be always true for at least the winner of the war, who will always claim their own good intentions, and always false for the loser. Further, if we can equate Moltmann's "good intentions" with moral intentions, then Hardt and Negri seem to question whether it is even possible to ever fulfill this condition: "Morality can only provide a solid basis to legitimate violence, authority, and domination when it refuses to admit different perspectives and judgments."[2]

The third condition cannot be evaluated until after the war is completed, which is quite impossible if we agree with Hardt and Negri that we are now living in a state of perpetual war. But, again, certainly one entering a war would *expect* conditions afterward to be better. Who would enter a war if they thought it would only

---

1 Ibid.

2 Hardt and Negri, 28.

make life worse? Similarly, condition five, concerning the means of war, is in the eye of the beholder.

The sixth and final condition, ensuring the safety of non-combatants, would seem to be an impossibility especially in these times of terrorist action when it is not easy to tell the difference between combatants and non-combatants and aggressors can be private transnational organizations instead of sovereign states. Nor can we claim self-defense as a justification for killing non-combatants. As Keller asserts, "Their violence against noncombatants will never justify ours."[1] One might argue that responses to terrorism do not constitute war but are more of a policing action. That may or may not be true, but even, and perhaps especially, in police actions there is a moral responsibility not to harm the innocent. Further, when our responses to terrorism involve invading or bombing foreign countries, as has been the case in Iraq and Afghanistan, those responses are then tantamount to waging war.

Only the fourth condition, exhausting all means of peaceful resolution, seems to hold out any hope at all and even that is at least partially in the eye of the beholder. Certainly, the U.S. government claimed all peaceful means had been tried before invading Iraq during the G.W. Bush administration.

It seems doubtful that there is any way to decide what constitutes a just war even if we could agree that a just war was a valid Christian response. Further, Hardt and Negri state, "The concept of justice serves to universalize war beyond any particular interests toward the interest of humanity as a whole."[2] If a war is just and waged in the name of justice, then the enemy can be demonized. "Along with the renewed concept of just war, then, comes also, predictably, the allied concept of evil. Posing the enemy as evil serves to make the enemy and the struggle against it absolute and thus outside of politics — evil is the enemy of all humanity."[3]

---

1 Keller, *God and Power*, 14.

2 Hardt and Negri, 15.

3 Ibid., 16.

If the war is "just," the enemy demonized, and the battle absolutized against evil then we have returned to an apocalyptic messianism which Keller says "must not only denounce its idolatry but disclose its self-contradiction. For the apocalypse and its Messiah are inherently *anti*-imperialist."[1] That is, an imperialist force cannot be the messiah that fights the apocalyptic battle against evil because the concepts of apocalypse and messiah are both inherently anti-imperialism. Moltmann concurs: "It cannot be maintained that any world empire is the goal of God's plan of deliverance for the peoples."[2]

Moltmann goes on to note that the idea of a just war in this nuclear age makes little sense: "As far as I am aware, no one in our European churches is a proponent of a 'just nuclear war,' because the limiting of such a war cannot be assured."[3] If a nuclear war cannot be limited, then it must be rejected outright, but Moltmann notes that this makes nuclear weapons useless even as a deterrence to others: "According to this doctrine, therefore, only the possession and threat, but not the use of nuclear weapons, may be allowed. If, however, one is not ready to use what one possesses, no deterrence results."[4] He believes that there seems to be no Christian reasoning that would even allow for the possession of such weapons: "If the use of the means of mass destruction is sin, then the *possession* of the means of mass destruction for the purpose of threatening and deterring the enemy cannot be justified as Christian."[5]

The concept of "just war" seems to hold little real hope for guidance. According to Moltmann, "We have reached the point, therefore, where we must go back and say that all war is irresponsible, is sin, and there can be no justification of it."[6] But, if the just

1 Keller, *God and Power*, 37.

2 Jürgen Moltmann, "Peacemaking and Dragonslaying in Christianity," in *The Politics of Discipleship and Discipleship in Politics*, ed. by Willard M. Swartley, 132-146 (Eugene, OR: Wipf & Stock Publishers, 2006), 137.

3 Moltmann, "Following Jesus," 58.

4 Ibid., 59.

5 Ibid., 67.

6 Ibid.

war concept doesn't help us find guidance as Christians to the problem of war, then is pacifism the answer? Can pacifism counter the imperial tendencies of the U.S. as well as the tyrannical impulses of many of those in power elsewhere in the world? Can violent tyrants be subverted with non-violence? Is pacifism *practical*? If it isn't, are we called to it anyway as Christians?

Moltmann states, "we must assume that *peace* is the order and promise of God."[1] We have already cast doubt on whether war and violence can ever be said to truly provide peace. However, can non-violence by only one side of a conflict ever produce peace? Or would it produce, as Keller noted, an unjust peace? Moltmann might be tempted to respond that there is no such thing as an unjust peace because "peace means not only the absence of war but also the overcoming of suffering, anxiety, threat, injustice, and oppression."[2] However important these additional goals are, they are not necessarily produced by pacifism. An absence of war and violence doesn't automatically solve suffering, injustice, and oppression.

Pacifism is not for the faint of heart. Noting that national security is "a politics of anxiety and fear,"[3] Moltmann admits that to pursue pacifism is to risk the security of yourself and the security of your nation: "Therefore whoever believes that nuclear war can be prevented only through unilateral disarmament... must risk the freedom, the rights and security of his or her own country in order to save the whole of life on this earth from nuclear death."[4] But for Moltmann it is the only option: "We deny God's peace when we secure ourselves before our enemies by becoming enemies to them, when we encounter their threat with counter-threat and their terror with horror."[5] "Pacifism is the only realism of life left to us in this apocalyptic situation of threatening world annihilation."[6]

1 Ibid., 56.
2 Ibid.
3 Ibid., 64.
4 Ibid., 62.
5 Ibid., 65.
6 Ibid., 69.

But, aren't there situations when violence and war are necessary, such as, to cite the classic example, when we are faced with a Hitler? Even Moltmann admits to being conflicted in this regard: "I do not represent the 'just war' teaching. I also do not advocate a justification of the murder of tyrants. But I know that there are situations in life in which one must resist and become guilty, in order to save human lives."[1]

Hardt and Negri, although holding peace up as the ideal of democracy,[2] seem even more willing to say that violence has a necessary place in countering violence: "Every exodus requires an active resistance, a rearguard war against the pursuing powers of sovereignty."[3] They also attempt to make a distinction between "a *democratic* use of force and violence" and "the war of sovereignty"[4] and then proceed to define the conditions of "democratic violence."[5] However, this seems to be nothing more than the just war principle under a different name in order to justify war as *they* desire.

Ultimately, Hardt and Negri, Moltmann, and Keller, all come back to love as the solution of war. Hardt and Negri, pinning their hopes on the democratic fervor of the "multitude," which they believe is what is developing as a post-modern society — a leaderless networked organization of people that maintains difference instead of forging a unified identity, say that "a concept of love is just what we need to grasp the constituent power of the multitude."[6] "Love serves as the basis for our political projects in common and this construction of a new society."[7] Moltmann states, "So, too, the love of enemies should overcome hostility and serve the common

1 Jürgen Moltmann, "A Response to the Responses," in *The Politics of Discipleship and Discipleship in Politics*, ed. Willard M. Swartley, 119-131 (Eugene, OR: Wipf & Stock Publishers, 2006), 130.
2 Hardt and Negri, 311.
3 Ibid., 342.
4 Ibid.
5 Ibid., 342-344.
6 Ibid., 351.
7 Ibid., 352.

good."[1] Keller adds, "It is not a harmless churchy balance of love and justice that we need, but an ekklesia (community) of just love, and eros that readies us for deadly dangers and for delightful surprises."[2]

Although as Christians we are indeed called to love, one must wonder whether love provides any kind of practical response to war. How is love a response to the Hitlers, the tyrants of the world who are interested only in their own power and wealth? It is hard to imagine that such psychopaths would very much care about or be influenced by love.

Our world is torn by war and violence. The concept of just war does not, when looked at closely, seem very just at all. Pacifism is a noble idea, but seems, at least in some circumstances, to be naïve. What then is the Christian response?

All Christians should be able to agree that war is tragic. War can never be said to be a good thing, but it is difficult to say that war is not sometimes necessary. How can we determine when war is necessary, while affirming that war is never "just"? War is not something to be entered into with enthusiasm or a sense of righteousness. I don't think it is possible to give generic principles as to when war is necessary or not. The principles of just war may be useful during such deliberations, but only if we keep in mind the fact that such generic principles can be manipulated to make any war seem justifiable, at least for a little while. As Christians dedicated to the principles of love, one might propose that we begin with a position of pacifism, knowing that at some time we may have no choice but to resort to the tragedies of war. In the meantime, however, both West and Moltmann offer some practical ideas on how we can at least minimize those times of no choice.

Moltmann believes that "*the service of peace* then must become the content of life in the community of Jesus Christ."[3] He offers three principles of what it means to be in the service of peace:

1 Moltmann, "Peacemaking," 144.

2 Keller, 111.

3 Moltmann, "Following Jesus," 67.

loving your enemy, recognizing and working to overcome the real dangers, and becoming a peace church.[1] For Moltmann, loving one's enemy includes not allowing hostility to be imposed upon us (that is, not automatically responding to violence with violence), recognizing the humanity of the other, and realizing the basis for hostilities.[2] Realizing this basis then becomes the work of solving the real problems of the world such as poverty and the destruction of the natural environment. The above principles, in fact, should be preconditions before any war could ever be called necessary.

Cornell West believes that "Socratic, prophetic, and tragicomic elements ... constitute the most sturdy democratic armor available to us in our fight against corrupt elite power."[3] These too need to be preconditions before any war could ever be called necessary. Meaningful dialog, prophetic witness to the ills of our world, and a catharsis of the soul through nonviolent means can all contribute to peace.

While war is a particularly heinous sin, we well know that it is not the only way we humans visit violence upon each other. We can look at history to see the devastating effects of slavery, concentration camps, and other instruments of violence that we have created to kill, oppress, and control those who differ from us. Even the church has been guilty in her history by conducting such atrocities as the medieval inquisitions. While oppressive violence is still conducted today, it is often more subtle as well. For example, ongoing racism and problems such as police brutality and biased sentencing in our judicial system often go unrecognized especially by those who are not the victims. Physical harm is not the only way to commit violence upon one another either. Continual anti-gay rhetoric, often perpetrated by the church, batters at our souls and results in abnormally high suicide rates among gay and lesbian youth. However, many of the principles of how we might respond

1 Ibid., 67-68.

2 Moltmann, "Peacemaking," 144-145.

3 West, 217.

to open warfare could also be applied to other forms of oppressive violence as well.

In response to the horrific communal and systemic sin of war or any use of oppressive violence, Christians absolutely must be committed to the principles of love. Following the practical steps of Moltmann and West in working for justice in the world in nonviolent ways can certainly bring a greater peace to the world. However, in our commitment to peace, we must also sadly admit that at times the tragedy of war, or violence in response to violence, may be necessary, but only as a last resort and only with a great sorrow for the death and destruction it brings to not only the tyrants of the world but also to the innocents.

Why Have You Forsaken Me: Suffering and Evil

Our inability to solve the problem of humanity's propensity to wage war is undeniably a source of suffering and evil in the world. In times such as these, many people lose faith in a Divine Presence that can seem to have no interest in our suffering. When things go wrong in life, we have a natural inclination to wonder why and question the role of the Divine Presence in these matters, which can range from the disappointing to the truly tragic. Globally, we might see it in the classic case of the 20th century Holocaust. In a church community, we might see it in a corporate bewilderment that a leap of faith, paying a new minister out of savings in the hope that it would lead to growth in the church, ends with an empty bank account and an acrimonious split in the congregation. Individually, we might see it in the experience of mothers whose children have died.

We ask ourselves the questions of theodicy: Why did the Divine Presence let these things happen? If the Divine Presence is good, why has this tragedy befallen us? It is a sentiment even expressed on the cross by Jesus when he quotes Psalm 22: "My God, my God, why have you forsaken me?"[1] The answers that are

1 Mark 15:34

typically offered, while they may be comforting to some, are unsatisfactory and often damaging. Sometimes we blame the victim, claiming they must have done something wrong or didn't pray hard enough or weren't faithful enough. Sometimes we claim it's a mystery, that we can't know the ways of the Divine Presence. Worse yet, sometimes we claim that tragedies are the will of the Divine and we should just accept it whether we understand it or not. On some level, all of these explanations sound like excuse-making on behalf of a divinity who just doesn't care.

Catherine Keller blames the "burden of godforsakenness" not on the suffering itself but on the "logic of omnipotence."[1] Theodicy cannot be approached, as is commonly done, with the presumption that the Divine Presence is omnipotent or all powerful. An omnipotent divinity necessarily leads to "well-meaning theological shibboleths like 'God's will is God's will' [which] can — and have — made suffering worse."[2]

An all-controlling divinity is antithetical to the idea of love[3] because, according to Keller, "love does not control. It opens a space of becoming."[4] If this is true, if love has more in common with freedom and growth than absolute control, then a divinity that is love could not be all-controlling and all powerful. An omnipotent, all powerful, all-controlling divinity will always lead us back to the Santa-for-adults God and away from the Divine Presence that is the electrifying pull of love. Tillich affirms this, noting that turning the Divine Presence into a divinity that can do whatever that divinity wants makes the Divine Presence into nothing more than a super-human being, a concept we have already rejected.[5] If we must speak of omnipotence, it might be best to follow Tillich's lead and redefine the word to say more about the Divine Presence's reach of power rather than strength of power. Modeling Tillich's

1 Keller, *Face of the Deep*, 215.
2 Keller, *On the Mystery*, 72.
3 Ibid., 79.
4 Ibid., 88.
5 Tillich, *Systematic Theology, Vol. 1*, 273.

definition, but with an understanding of the multiplicity of the Divine Presence and all that implies, we might define omnipotence as the power of love which resists separation in all its expressions and which is manifest in the multiplicity of incarnation in all its forms.[1] That is, the "omni" in omnipotence refers to the fact that the pull of love toward reunion is present in *all* things. Omnipotence becomes omnipresence, a far-reaching power of influencing action and not all-controlling action.

If the common understanding of omnipotence is rejected in favor of this new one, then the concept of godforsakenness is also rejected. The Divine Presence never truly leaves us — it cannot. But neither can it fix all of our problems. Instead, the Divine Presence suffers with us. For Sally McFague, if we understand the world as part of the Divine Presence, then "the evil in the world, all kinds of evil, occurs in and to God as well as to us and the rest of creation."[2] The Divine Presence does not cause or initiate suffering or evil, but, as the electrifying pull of love, is the "negative critique of them."[3] Keller states that "the biblical vision requires a God who suffers with our suffering, who shares our vulnerability"[4] and uses Jesus' death as an example: "God is there with Jesus on the cross. Sure. Not as the one who wills the atrocity as a means to the good. But otherwise: as the one who is indeed in Jesus, suffering what he suffers."[5] It is in this co-suffering that the Divine Presence continues to call us to loving reunion, luring good from evil.[6]

The Divine Presence does not cause suffering or rescue us from it.[7] However, a creation which allows for freedom, not only for the

---

1 Ibid. Tillich's definition of omnipotence is "the power of being which resists nonbeing in all its expressions and which is manifest in the creative process in all its forms." It is interesting to note the multiplicity that one might discern in Tillich's words.

2 McFague, *Models of God*, 72.

3 McFague, *A New Climate*, 172.

4 Keller, *On the Mystery*, 127.

5 Ibid., 86.

6 Ibid.

7 Keller, *Face of the Deep*, 220.

human but for all, holds the possibility of suffering and evil. Shit happens: to both bad people and good, to the morally bankrupt and the righteous, to the worst sinner and even to Jesus, the epitome of union with the love of the Divine Presence. Sometimes suffering happens for no understandable reason, sometimes by unintentional actions, and sometimes it is caused by despicably intentional human action. In the midst of these risks of suffering, the Divine Presence calls us to new places, to learn from the tragedies of life. The Divine Presence not only suffers with us, but continually pulls us toward reunion, toward love, toward new opportunity and toward new creation.[1]

1 Ibid.

Chapter 5 Discussion Questions

1. How are humans separated from the Divine Presence, each other, and Creation? What are some of the ways we can re-connect?
2. What systemic sin (i.e. separation) do you encounter in your life? What are the messages and actions taken by our culture and institutions that reinforce and encourage this sin?
3. Under what conditions is war justified? In what ways can we act in love that might prevent or reduce violence in our world?
4. In what ways have you experienced the Divine Presence acting in your life? In what ways have you ever felt the Divine Presence as absent in your life?
5. Have you ever felt the Divine Presence as suffering with you in difficult moments?
6. In a moment of tragedy, where might we see the Divine Presence other than in a controlling role?

Counter it: Speak to the injustice when it happens! Call each other on it.

6 A Light for the World

Thoughts on Christ

One Night in Bethlehem: Jesus as Incarnation

If we are to live out of a Christian paradigm, claiming to be followers of Jesus, then we need to come to terms with who Jesus was and what the stories of his life and his teachings mean to us and for us. In churches, such as my own, which place a high value on questioning one finds divergent understandings of Jesus. For some he is a savior, but for others he is more simply a wise teacher or a model of how we should live our lives. Some understand him as both divine and human and for others Jesus was no different in his essence than any other person.

In the early days of my own church, Phoenix Community Church, some of the people felt so deeply wounded by Christianity that they had difficulty incorporating the figure of Jesus into their spirituality. Jesus is not mentioned at all in the church's long standing mission statement and a former minister once joked that she had to stub her toe just to be able to mention Jesus' name in church. Today, those who constitute this local congregation more readily accept a Christian identity, however they define that personally, and its corresponding Jesus-talk.

In the church's current expression of core beliefs Jesus is equated with love. The church's statement of purpose says the church is "to embody God's all encompassing love, as exemplified by Jesus."[1] If any claim regarding Jesus can be made on behalf of Phoenix Community Church, it might be found in Patrick Cheng's affirmations that Jesus is "the *embodiment of radical love*, or radical love

1 "Our Purpose Statement," http://www.phoenixchurch.org/mission.php (accessed 30 May 2016).

made flesh,"[1] and that Jesus reveals the true nature of the Divine Presence, which is love itself, through that embodiment.[2]

Jesus the person is an "historically cloudy figure,"[3] whom we know through Biblical gospels which often vary on details, conflict with each other and present his story through particular agendas for particular audiences. We even hear debates today about whether Jesus even existed as a living, breathing figure in history. Although I tend to believe there was an historical Jesus upon which the gospels are based, it is certainly unclear how accurately the gospel accounts recount the actual events of his life. Ultimately, I don't think it matters. The truths of Christianity are based on a set of stories about Jesus and teachings attributed to Jesus (as well as others such as the apostle Paul). Even if it was proven beyond a shadow of a doubt that an historical Jesus never existed, such a revelation, while it would be shocking to many, would not change the underlying truths of Christianity at all.

Although there is little we can be sure of regarding the historical human named Jesus, Christian tradition tells us that one night in the small town of Bethlehem, the Divine Presence became flesh in the body of a small child named Jesus. This child then grew up, came to have a ministry through which many understood him to be the Messiah or Christ (that is, anointed by the Divine Presence to be a savior of the people) and who was then crucified by the Romans. In the Christian claim that Jesus is the Christ, he becomes the central revelation of Christianity as the incarnation of the Divine Presence in earthly flesh. Sallie McFague stresses that Jesus is not the first or the last incarnation of the Divine Presence in the world, but is the revelation of Divine incarnation that allows us to understand that the Divine Presence is in all the world, all the time.[4] Similarly, Paul Tillich, while not discounting other or

1 Cheng, *Radical Love*, 78.

2 Cheng, *From Sin to Amazing Grace*, 81.

3 Kenneth Arthur, *The Queer Christ: Recognizing Ourselves in the Divine* (Chicago: Chicago Theological Seminary, Master of Arts thesis, 2009), 47.

4 McFague, *A New Climate*, 72.

* why no mention of ~ resurrection

ongoing revelations, asserts that Jesus is the decisive revelation[1] who shows us "the essential unity" of the human being and the Divine Presence.[2] As the incarnation of the Divine in human flesh, Jesus the Christ definitively reveals the true divine nature of humanity and all of creation, as it has always been and always will be.

According to Cheng, the Divine Presence and humanity come together in the person of Jesus the Christ[3] and in doing so break down "the boundaries of divine vs. human."[4] That is, Jesus the Christ, as the incarnation of the Divine Presence, is not only a revelation of that Divine Presence, but also reveals the Divine Presence within all humans. Because any assumed boundary between human flesh and the Divine is clearly removed for Jesus, it allows us to see that this boundary really does not exist for anyone or any part of creation. As previously quoted, Catherine Keller states that "the grandeur" in the incarnation of the Divine Presence in Jesus the Christ "lies precisely in its illumination of the word enfleshed in every creature of the creation."[5] Jesus reveals that the Divine Presence which is incarnated in Jesus is incarnated "always and everywhere," not just in humanity but in all of creation.[6] Human beings have always shared a deep fundamental connection with the Divine Presence, each other and creation because the Divine resides in us and all things[7] and connects us even in our fleshy state of separation.

Loving the World: Jesus' Life and Ministry

The incarnation of the Divine Presence in the world affirms the importance of our fleshy universe. As "earthly creatures" we "live and move and have our being" in the Divine Presence, which,

1 Tillich, *Systematic Theology, Vol. 1*, 133.
2 Tillich, *Systematic Theology, Vol. 2*, 122.
3 Cheng, *Radical Love*, 79.
4 Cheng, *Rainbow Theology*, 139.
5 Keller, *On The Mystery*, 152.
6 Ibid., 151.
7 Ephesians 4:6

according to McFague, shows that "God is not anti-flesh or anti-world; in fact just the opposite."[1] The incarnation shows us that the world is to be loved because the Divine Presence loves it. The problem "becomes figuring out what loving the world means."[2]

Christians sometimes seem to focus exclusively on the symbols of Jesus' incarnation or his death and resurrection. Believing in the historicity of those events and their institutionally approved interpretations becomes the sole means of our salvation. However, we shouldn't ignore Jesus' life and ministry in favor of these powerful and meaningful symbols. While in his essential being Jesus the Christ reveals that the love which is the Divine Presence is incarnate in all things, in his life and ministry he demonstrates, in a more practical sense, what it means to be that love in human form. Most of Jesus' life, most of his time as the physical fleshy incarnation of love, was spent interacting with people while teaching and healing, trying to change hearts and minds to build the kin-dom of the Divine Presence here on this earth, a better world of hope, peace and justice. That is, in addition to the symbolism of his birth, death and resurrection, Jesus the Christ showed us through the words and actions of his life what loving the world truly means.

Part of loving the world is creating and nurturing community and meaningful relationships. Jesus showed us how to love the world, as McFague says, by manifesting "in his own life and death that the heart of the universe is unqualified love working to befriend the needy, the outcast, the oppressed."[3] To love the world is to care for those in need, to care about creating a just world. To love the world is also to care about the fleshy health of the world and not only save its inhabitants for some later, higher spiritual realm.

Keller notes that "Jesus was simply not interested in people's relations to God in abstraction from their relation to others."[4] For example, along with his proclamation of the kin-dom, however

1 McFague, *A New Climate*, 34.

2 Ibid.

3 McFague, *Models of God*, 55.

4 Keller, *On the Mystery*, 143.

we understand that, Jesus also healed the sick.[1] He was profoundly concerned about the plight of people in this earthly world. In the gospel of Luke, Jesus begins his ministry by reading from the book of Isaiah, declaring he was sent to bring good news to the poor, "proclaim release to the captives and recovery of sight to the blind, to let the oppressed go free."[2]

When Jesus the Christ taught that to love the Divine Presence and our neighbors as ourselves was the "greatest commandment,"[3] it is reasonable to conclude from his life's example that he meant we should love our neighbor and ourselves by truly caring about our plight here on this earth in all of the fleshiness of life. In the gospel of Luke the commandment to love our neighbor is even illustrated by the parable we know as the story of the "Good Samaritan," in which a Samaritan cares for an injured man who was supposed to be his enemy, thus showing us quite clearly that loving our neighbor means addressing each other's needs in the here and now.[4] That is, we should love not just emotionally but with an active compassion, a suffering-with, that envisions and works toward a world where all people, and all of creation, may find not only love, but a kin-dom of hope, peace, and justice.

The Queer Christ: Jesus as Multiplicity

In showing us what loving the world means, Christ is the light which illuminates the picture of human wholeness which we seek, which is to embrace and be reunited with the Divine, the electrifying power of love that permeates the universe. While the Spirit of the Divine Presence within us guides us to wholeness as individuals, it is to Christ that the Spirit points as the model. As

1 Matthew 4:23. There are numerous accounts of Jesus healing in the canonical gospels. See the next section on eschatology for additional discussion of the kin-dom, which can be understood as being as much or more about this world than a heavenly realm.

2 Luke 4:18.

3 Matthew 22:36-40 and Mark 12:28-31

4 Luke 10:25-37

Tillich states, Jesus the Christ shows us what the Divine Presence desires humanity to be and what the human being "essentially is and therefore ought to be."[1] In becoming Christ-like through embracing our own divine nature and living a life of love by embracing and caring for each of the sacred parts of creation, including but not limited to human beings, we approach reunion with the Divine and grow toward wholeness.

But Jesus the Christ does more than reveal to us an image of what *an ideal* human looks like. That is, he does not present us with a single picture to which we must all adhere. Instead, Christ "is a symbol of multiplicity — and not singularity."[2] Jesus the Christ shows us that the Divine Presence is in all things by breaking through the human-divine boundary. As the ultimate model of what humanity is and can be, he reveals to us the many and diverse ways the Divine manifests in humans, appearing "to us in a multiplicity of ways."[3]

One way Christ appears to us as a multiplicity is through the theological images we use to talk about and understand his impact on our life. These images morph or shape-shift into the revelation that is needed by the recipient. Examples include such images as the Black Christ, the Asian Christ, and the Queer Christ.[4] This is one instance where (partially) personifying the Divine Presence through images of the Christ makes sense because these images of Christ "help provide new meaning to those unsure about the relevance of Christ or who have rejected or been rejected by the church."[5] Of course, the Queer Christ is of particular interest to queer people who don't conform to cultural norms of heterosexuality. Just as

1 Tillich, *Systematic Theology, Vol. 2*, 93.

2 Cheng, *Rainbow Theology*, 146.

3 Ibid., 147.

4 It may be helpful to think of the Christ here as the archetypal messiah or anointed one of the Divine Presence rather than the human being named Jesus who lived about two thousand years ago. The difference is subtle but significant. Jesus was the Christ but Jesus as the Christ transcends the human named Jesus.

5 Arthur, 3.

"Jesus Christ says that he takes the form of the least among us," the Queer Christ is the particular image of Christ as a marginalized queer person.[1] Just as the image of a Black Christ suggests that Christ and the gospel message is not just for white people, the Queer Christ emphasizes that the gospel is not just for heterosexual people.[2] The Queer Christ "transgresses the boundaries of the male heterosexual/asexual Christ model traditionally presented by the figure of Jesus"[3] and helps to "undermine the oppressive power of institutional Christianity"[4] in their treatment of the marginalized.

This is the Christ that stands up for anyone who has ever felt they don't belong. The Queer Christ is important because it allows us to recognize "ourselves in Christ and the Christ in ourselves," thus helping to further reveal the divinity of all people, and especially queer people, and affirm our inherent worth and the "spiritual treasures" to be found within each of us.[5] For queer people to identify with the Queer Christ and find meaning in that image, we must understand the Queer Christ as "a fully human, imperfect, sexual Christ who is still fully divine and not necessarily male."[6] Because the Christian church has so often told queer people that they are not fully human, the queer Christian must be able to see their full humanity in Christ in order to know the fallacy of that teaching.[7] We must know that the Queer Christ struggled as we struggle, truly understanding the queer person, and yet lived in harmony with the Divine Presence not in spite of his queerness but because of it. The Queer Christ in whom we can see our true human potential is "a great hope for all of humanity" and not just queer people.[8] In disrupting the image of the heterosexual / asexual gender-conforming Christ that reinforces the doctrine of the

1 Cheng, *Rainbow Theology*, 147. See also Matthew 25.
2 Arthur, 2.
3 Ibid., 4.
4 Ibid., 17.
5 Ibid.
6 Ibid., 27.
7 Ibid., 25.
8 Ibid., 31.

Everyone-must-be-like-me God, the Queer Christ opens access to the Divine Presence to not only queer people but all people who fail to conform in some way. In so doing, the Queer Christ enriches all of us by lifting up and celebrating the diversity and sacredness of all of the Divine Presence's good creation.

Another way Christ appears to us as multiplicity is as the face of the other, the face of those who are not like us. The face of the other is present in the Queer Christ, which can hopefully jar us out of our selfish complacency and reveal the injustice of the church's treatment of queer people.[1] Christ as part of the Trinity also reveals the face of the other. Representing the multiplicity of the Divine Presence as incarnated in creation, he becomes a reminder of the Divine Presence within our neighbors, affirming at the same time that we are both diverse individuals and connected at the level of our very being, and calling out to us for justice and love in our relationships. Jesus himself tells us that how we act toward the hungry, the stranger and the prisoner is the same as acting toward Jesus.[2] Indeed, how we act toward the marginalized and oppressed is the same as acting toward the Divine Presence. Ignore those in need and we ignore Christ. Help those in need and we help Christ.

On the Cross: Salvation

Easter, the time of remembering the death and resurrection of Jesus the Christ, is arguably the most significant religious season in the worshipping life of Phoenix Community Church. The church's traditional Good Friday Tenebrae service is perhaps the most anticipated worship service of the year. This resonance with the Easter season is understandable for a people who have felt a measure of suffering and rejection in their lives and yet wish to live out of the hope implied in the church's name, which refers to the mythical Phoenix bird rising to new life out of the ashes of death.

While many of the people of Phoenix Community Church would be able to identify with the suffering of the crucified Jesus,

1 Ibid., 46.

2 Matthew 25:31-46

most would reject the idea that this suffering was some kind of penance or punishment required by the Divine Presence, which would imply their own suffering was also divinely required. According to the theologian JoAnne Marie Terrell, such understandings of sacrifice derived from Jesus' crucifixion have historically been used by the church "on subjugated peoples in order to justify the abusive policies of the state and its own ministerium."[1] That is, the uplifting of torturous suffering as a blessed sacrifice has been used to justify oppression by also making it a noble sacrifice, which is clearly contrary to the life and ministry of Jesus which was spent trying to relieve the suffering of the oppressed. But, if Jesus' death was not a divinely pre-planned sacrifice, then how are we to understand it and its central role in Christianity?

Pamela Dickey Young rejects any divine role in Jesus' death, claiming that "the suffering and death that happened to Jesus are the product of human evil not of divine will."[2] For her, Jesus' death is not something that is to be revered but is to "be resisted as evil."[3] Marcus Borg and John Dominic Crossan understand Jesus' death as something that was not necessary, but was inevitable because death was simply something that happened to those who challenged Roman power in the first century.[4] Rejecting any Divine plan in connection with Jesus' torturous death, the death becomes a seemingly unnecessary tragedy that most humans can identify with. It is in a pointless death that Jesus, along with us, can ask why the Divine Presence has forsaken him. It is in a pointless death that Jesus, even as the incarnation of the Divine Presence itself, becomes one who suffers with us and not for us. That intimate knowledge of human tragedy can reassure us even today that the Divine Presence

1 JoAnne Marie Terrell, *Power in the Blood? The Cross in the African American Experience*, (Eugene, Oregon: Wipf & Stock Publishers, 2005), 107.

2 Pamela Dickey Young, "Beyond Moral Influence to an Atoning Life," *Theology Today* Vol. 52 Issue 3 (October 1995), 353.

3 Ibid.

4 Borg and Crossan, 161.

walks with us in our own trials and provides us with the hope of one who has known tragedy and triumphed.

If our talk of Jesus ended with his earthly end, then his death might remain pointless. However, the Good News of Christianity is largely based on the fantastical claim that Jesus' death was not his end, but that he was resurrected. For McFague, "the resurrection is a way of speaking about an awareness that the presence of God in Jesus is a permanent presence in our present."[1] Through the resurrection Jesus the human being is declared to truly be Jesus the Christ, whom he in fact was since his incarnation as a human child and continues to be for us today as an ongoing and meaningful force in our lives.

The resurrection of Christ is a revelation meant to teach and remind us of the new life that the Divine Presence brings out of death. Resurrection is the Divine's promise of new life, that it is possible to rise out of the ashes of despair. When life seems bleak, it asks us to trust that anything is possible. It is the promise of eternal hope: that nothing, not even death, can separate us from the love that is the Divine Presence. Resurrection looks into the void of human expectations and asks us to see life where previously we saw only death and decay. It asserts that ultimately more powerful than the greedy and violent ways of the world is the way of the Divine Presence, a path of active and unconditional love and compassion. Resurrection proclaims that love conquers fear and hate, now and always.

While resurrection may also speak to a life after our physical deaths, it is, more importantly, about our life in the here and now. Resurrection is available to us every day and not only upon our deaths. It is a promise that we too can break out of our own symbolic tombs. Because the electrifying pull of love that is the Divine Presence cannot be stopped, not even by the most powerful force we know — death — we know that we can break forth from the tombs that we build around ourselves, whether they be constructed from worry, fear, expectations of others, low self-esteem, or

1 McFague, *Models of God*, 59.

anything else, and live fully and abundantly as healed and whole manifestations of the Divine.

Jesus the Christ is the promise and revelation of the reality of resurrection. As humans, we may seem content at times with a dead life, a zombie-like existence that buries us under the tombstones of decay and corruption, that manifests racism, sexism, misogyny, and homophobia, that is built upon fear and hate. The Divine Presence, however, wants us to roll away those stones that threaten to keep us buried and breathe new life into us, to create in us the possibility of hope and peace not only for ourselves but for the world as well.[1]

Proclaiming the resurrection of Jesus is partly about choosing our attitude toward life. It's a giving-in to the pull of love, a trusting in the reality of the way of the Divine Presence. It means seeing the promise of new life when all appears hopeless and choosing love in the face of fear and hate. In this way, resurrection helps guide us toward healing and wholeness, toward salvation.

The resurrection declares that Jesus the Christ is savior, but according to Tillich this is not a savior whose sole purpose is to help humans escape hell and reach heaven.[2] Salvation instead means achieving wholeness in this earthly life. It means being healed through reunion with the Divine Presence. Christ as the savior "makes 'heal and whole' what is sick and disrupted."[3] Salvation means bridging the gap between the Divine and humanity, "bridging the infinite gap between the infinite and the finite."[4]

As we seek the Divine, the Divine Presence reaches out to us through Jesus the Christ, who shows us the path to healing and wholeness. For those who choose to seek the Divine Presence from within the Christian path, reunion with the Divine partly comes through following the example of Jesus' life and his teachings. However, for Tillich, Jesus the Christ is the word, or logos, and

---

1 Lewis, Karoline, "True Resurrection," http://www.workingpreacher.org/craft.aspx?post=4571 (accessed 30 May 2016).

2 Tillich, *Eternal Now*, 114.

3 Ibid., 113.

4 Tillich, *Systematic Theology Vol. 2*, 93.

as such it is not just his life and ministry but his entire being that matters,[1] including his birth, or incarnation, and its corresponding revelations, as well as his death and resurrection. Through the Christ as logos, through his total being, Keller says that "at all times and in all places, the logos offers a lure, a possibility, a new chance, for our becoming" what we are meant to be.[2] Jesus the Christ offers us the hope and possibility of reunion with the Divine Presence by revealing to us what is possible and acting as our guide on our own path of becoming.

Through bodily resurrection from his suffering and death, Christ calls us to loving reunion with the Divine Presence even in what seems to be our darkest moments, affirming earthly life and giving us hope of our own resurrection in the midst of our most profound difficulties. In a sense, Christ is in the business of resurrecting others. This resurrection or giving of life by Jesus the Christ is not just a resurrection after physical death. As Tillich explains, Christ "does not save individuals in a path leading out of historical existence; he is to transform historical existence. The individual enters a new reality which embraces society and nature."[3] That is, salvation is about this world we live in now and not about going to heaven.

Likewise, we can understand resurrection not as spiritual life after physical death but as resurrection from the many little deaths that we experience while alive. Life itself is a continual process of death and resurrection, letting go of the old and irrelevant in favor of new life. Faith in Jesus as the Christ is the trust that resurrection will always follow death. Tillich points out that "God does not leave the world at any place, in any time, without saviours — without healing power."[4] Just as the Divine Presence heals and liberates through Jesus the Christ, healing and liberation comes in many ways including through our own lives.

1 Tillich, *Systematic Theology Vol. 1*, 158.

2 Keller, *On the Mystery*, 149.

3 Tillich, *Systematic Theology Vol. 2*, 88.

4 Tillich, *Eternal Now*, 116.

This healing and liberation that we can find in Jesus the Christ and that we can help bring to the world is not just for certain individuals, either. Because the Divine Presence, humanity, and creation are all deeply connected, salvation should also be understood as universal or intended for everyone and everything. Tillich states that "we are saved not as individuals, but in unity with all others and with the universe."[1] Keller stresses that "Salvation, from salvus, meaning health, well-being, wholeness, cannot take place for one part of a body while the rest is ill."[2] Part of being healed is realizing that our own welfare is indivisible from the welfare of "those inconspicuous others huddled at the margins of [our] vision."[3]

As the face of the other and the definitive revelation of the Divine within the world, Jesus the Christ brings healing and liberation not just to individuals but to communities and to all of creation. As beings interconnected with the Divine Presence, each other and creation, what affects one of us affects all of us. It is for this reason we need to heed the call of the Divine Presence, the electrifying pull of love, to care for each other and the world.

Returning to the Divine: Seeking Forgiveness

Jesus' death on the cross is often associated with salvation through the forgiveness of sins in a theory of substitutionary atonement. The theory proposes that we are so terrible that we deserve to be punished for our sins in an everlasting hell, but Jesus took our punishment upon himself that we might be saved from this fate. In that way, the theory goes, Jesus died for the forgiveness of our sins. Of course, we have already rejected the premise of this theory, that humans are inherently evil, as un-Biblical and contrary to our experience of life and the Divine Presence. Therefore the theory itself must be rejected. In fact, Jesus' death in no way helped to bring about the forgiveness of sins. If anything, it was itself a sin

1 Ibid., 121.
2 Keller, *On the Mystery*, 144-145.
3 Ibid., 144.

+ Sin as separation / estrangement

— an act by the worldly powers of his day that further separated the world from the Divine Presence.

However, we could argue that almost everything else about Jesus was about the forgiveness of sin. He was born into this world, lived a ministry of love and healing and was resurrected from death all to reveal to us a path to reunion, a path to full and intimate relationship with the Divine Presence. In other words, everything about Jesus was so that our sin may be forgiven, that our estrangement from the Divine may be healed. And, while everything about Jesus the Christ's very existence carries the assurance of the Divine's forgiveness for us, we are often trapped by our inability to forgive ourselves and each other.

In many ways, our relationship with the Divine Presence is reflected in the relationships we have with each other. Jesus teaches that the essence of Divine law is to love the Divine Presence and to love our neighbor as ourselves. Everything else derives from this command. We can't be right with the Divine if we're not doing everything we can to be right with each other, our neighbors, and we can't be right with our neighbors if we aren't also seeking to be right with the Divine Presence.

In his ministry, Jesus talks about our relationship in community and how we are to restore that relationship when it is broken.[1] In other words, he talks about how we are to respond to our sin, our separation from each other and from the Divine. Jesus tells us that where two or three are gathered, where community is gathered in his name, Jesus is there as well. And he promises that if we agree in prayer on something then the Divine Presence will grant that prayer. This is not a guarantee that we will get whatever we want, as if the Divine Presence were granting us wishes. This would simply be returning to the Santa-for-adults God. It is, I think, a promise that when we are in agreement, when we are in right relationship with each other and when we come to the Divine Presence in that right relationship, then anything is possible.

1 Matthew 18:15-35

We know that sometimes being in community is difficult. We disagree with each other. We even hurt each other. However, Jesus doesn't say he is present when two or three people who agree with each other gather in his name. He asserts simply that where two or three gather in his name, he will also be present. It is important to know that Jesus is with us, loving us, guiding us, and supporting us even when our relationships with one another may seem broken. The followers of the Divine Presence are community. We're on this journey together, linked together, even in our disagreements, and even when we hurt each other.

We will experience broken relationships because we are human. When this happens, we're supposed to talk and listen to each other, to understand each other, that we may be restored. Of course, we may need someone to observe and help us resolve our differences. Jesus says if we can't work it out on our own, then take two or three witnesses with us and if we still can't be reconciled and restored, then it is a matter for the whole community because broken relationships affect all of the community.

We are all connected with each other and with the Divine. If a spider web is broken, then the whole thing is less effective. Likewise, if there is a hole in a net, then it doesn't serve its function as well as it should. It needs to be mended. It needs to be restored. So it is with our relationships. We don't necessarily need to always agree with each other. We shouldn't expect life and our relationships to be without bumps. But we need to talk. We need to listen. We need to communicate. We need to be in healthy relationship with each other and with the Divine Presence. We need to be in community.

Jesus goes on to tell us, "whatever you bind on earth will be bound in heaven, and whatever you loose on earth will be loosed in heaven."[1] There is an intimate connection between what we say and do, our relationships with each other, and our spiritual lives, our relationship with the Divine Presence. How we treat each other is how we treat the Divine Presence. To live in the love of the Divine,

1 Matthew 18:18

to manifest love in our lives, is to love each other with the same unconditional love that we receive from the Divine Presence. To be cut off or separated from each other is to be cut off or separated from the Divine.

To live in the love of the Divine doesn't require we all agree with each other all the time. But it does mean that when relationships are broken, we need to seek forgiveness, we need to seek restoration, authentically, from the heart. Peter realizes this and asks Jesus, "how often should I forgive? As many as seven times?" To which Jesus replies, "Not seven times, but, I tell you, seventy-seven times" (or in some translations, seventy times seven times).[1]

Forgiveness is a critical component of restoring relationships. Forgiveness is meant to be transformative. It opens up a future where there doesn't seem to be one and declares that the past need not dictate the future. Forgiveness has remarkable power. We may remember the story from a few years ago when a man murdered a group of Amish school children and then killed himself. I was utterly amazed when that Amish community, the families of those murdered children, reached out to the man's widow and offered forgiveness. It seems to me to be such an incredible act of courage for those families to forgive instead of holding onto pain and bitterness. But doing so transformed a situation where there must have seemed no way forward for either the widow or the families into a situation where they could at least glimpse a future.

Most of us probably know from our own lives how hard it can be to forgive not only the tragic wrongs but even the little hurts in life. But this is why forgiveness is a spiritual practice, with an emphasis on practice. To forgive seventy times seven times is to forgive from the depths of the Divine's mercy. It's an endless abundance of forgiveness: absolute, complete, and beyond counting. It means when we can't forgive, we keep forgiving anyway. We forgive until it wears down our walls of pain, hate, and bitterness. Each time we make an effort to forgive is like taking a hammer to those walls. Even if they don't come down at first, Jesus tells us to keep

1 Matthew 18:21-2

forgiving, keep hammering, until the walls are gone, until the way to restoration is clear.

To be clear, forgiveness is not about subjecting ourselves to continued hurt or abuse. Jesus tells us to confront those who are hurting us. We cannot forgive a hurt until the hurting has stopped. Forgiveness is not about hiding our pain, either. True forgiveness requires acknowledging our pain and seeking restoration in the midst of that pain. It is the desire to recognize that the future need not be controlled by the past, to refuse to let that pain rule our hearts.

To forgive seventy times seven times is to practice forgiving until it becomes ingrained in our very souls. To forgive from our hearts is to make love the ruler of our hearts, not our pain and bitterness. For what we declare bound on earth will be bound in heaven and what we loose on earth will be loosed in heaven. If pain and bitterness rule our earthly relationships, they will also rule our relationship with the Divine Presence. But if love and forgiveness rule our earthly relationships, then they will rule our relationship with the Divine Presence.

This is, perhaps, what Jesus was getting at in the parable of the servant who owed a large sum of money to the king.[1] The king was ready to forgive him a debt of unimaginable proportions, the equivalent in our times to tens or even hundreds of millions of dollars. But so forgiven, the servant couldn't then forgive one who was indebted to him for a paltry sum, maybe a few thousand dollars (depending on how we translate those sums). Not being able to extend the forgiveness given to him, the servant lost the forgiveness he had received and was handed over to be tortured until he was able to repay the debt.

The servant's fate in this parable is not some kind of warning of eternal punishment or hell, but it is instead a warning of the real way in which the inability to forgive from the heart, to forgive and mean it, can torture us. If we let the pain and bitterness of all the ways we are hurt in this life rule us we only torture ourselves. But if we take seriously the need to forgive and keep forgiving until it

1 Matthew 18:23-34

takes hold in our hearts, if we forgive seventy times seven times, if we forgive from the heart, then we can free ourselves from the grip of the past and make possible the restoration of both our earthly relationships and our relationship with the Divine Presence.

There will be times when forgiveness seems impossible. It may take us time to truly forgive. It may even require seeking help from a minister or therapist or trusted friend. Jesus also recognizes that despite our best efforts, perhaps not all broken relationships can be repaired. We are told that if we try everything and nothing works, if we still can't reconcile ourselves, if we still are not able to listen to each other, then we should treat those with whom our relationship is broken as a Gentile or a tax collector. These are people who were treated with suspicion and dislike in Jesus' culture. People who were shunned. That is how I've read this scripture in the past: if you try everything and nothing works, then forget them and move on with your life.

But is that what Jesus is really saying? Shunning may be how the culture treated Gentiles and tax collectors, but Jesus sought out those who were supposed to be the outsiders and outcasts. He ate with them. He hung out with them. He talked with them. He treated them with love. Jesus telling us to treat as Gentiles and tax collectors those with whom we can't find a way to be reconciled carries with it an ambiguity of rejection and special invitation. Even when we can't find restoration, we are called to continue to love each other, to continue to reach out to each other. We are called to gather as a community living and manifesting the love of the Divine Presence, a community that is not afraid of the hard work of relationship building, a community that seeks to mend the brokenness between each other and between us and the Divine Presence, a forgiving, restoring community.

It is Jesus the Christ, whose life and ministry was dedicated to forgiveness, who calls us to recognize the divinity in ourselves and in the face of the other. Jesus, who breaks down the barriers between divinity and humanity, lights the way for us, showing us what it means to love so that, in our glorious diversity, we may be united in new life and made whole.

Chapter 6 Discussion Questions

1. How would you describe Jesus in terms of his relationship with the Divine Presence? What is Jesus to us here in the 21st Century?
2. What does Jesus' life and teachings tell us about how we should live and act toward each other and Creation? How are we falling short of that? How are we living up to Jesus' example?
3. In what ways do you see Christ (and/or the Divine Presence) in other people, including strangers or people you don't know well?
4. Do you think Jesus' death was mandated by the Divine Presence? Why or why not? What does your answer imply about the nature of the Divine?
5. What does the concept of resurrection mean to you and your own spiritual journey?
6. Why is it sometimes so hard to forgive others or even ourselves? What can we do in the face of that difficulty?

7 Realizing the Kin-dom

Thoughts on The End Times

Ultimate Mystery: The Kin-dom in Heaven

Sometimes it seems as if Christians are obsessed with the end of things, both our individual ends as well as the end of the world as we know it. We're fascinated with near-death experiences and enthralled by predictions of the so-called rapture, while television preachers frighten us with great detail about why they believe these "end times" are right around the corner. We want to know what our ultimate fate will be, collectively and individually. Is there life after death? Is there a heaven and hell? If so, what are they like? Many of us have developed an elaborate image of what our end will look like. We explain in detail what we will experience after our physical body finally fails us and make bold predictions of the end of the world.

However, what we are really asking when we contemplate our ultimate fate is "why?" Why are we here? What is the end goal, the purpose, of our existence? In a sense, our reflections up to this point have already proposed an answer to that question: the work and hope of human existence is to find our wholeness, our reunion with the Divine Presence. This is the goal which provides meaning to our existence. For Christians this reunion is sought through Christ as the revelation and model of our wholeness, showing us what it means to be reunited with the Divine, and the Holy Spirit is our guide along the journey. Patrick Cheng understands eschatology, or the "doctrine of last things," to be about this reunion, which is "the ultimate return" to the love out of which we were created.[1] The

1 Cheng, *Radical Love*, 131.

vision of the end times is the vision of what it means to be fully at one with the Divine Presence which is the electrifying pull of love.

Another way to talk about the eschaton, the final event that is the ultimate and universal reunion with the Divine presence, is to talk about achieving the Kin-dom of the Divine Presence. The Kin-dom was the end goal of Jesus' ministry. Jesus went about the countryside "proclaiming the good news of the kingdom"[1] and he was often telling parables that were meant to illustrate what the Kin-dom was like. It, in fact, is the eschaton. It represents the Divine Presence's ultimate goal for all of Creation: that we be reunited in Divine love.

It is important that we understand, as Sallie McFague and Paul Tillich both do, that the reunion with the Divine is a process that includes all of creation.[2] Humanity cannot find wholeness if we continue to abuse the Divine's good creation that we live in. This, I hope, is reflected in the phrase I am choosing to use, Kin-dom, instead of the more traditional term kingdom. A kingdom is a place where an hierarchal patriarchy rules with total power. To talk of a kingdom may have made sense in times past when kingdoms were the assumed order of the world and we understood the Divine to be the Santa-for-adults God or the Everyone-must-be-like-me God. However, having evolved past those understandings, we need to affirm that it cannot be to a kingdom that we are being led. The term Kin-dom offers an alternative vision of what this ultimate reunion with the Divine looks like. Instead of lifting up hierarchal patriarchy as our ultimate end, it emphasizes our relationship with the rest of Creation using kin, or a family concept, as a metaphor. Like our kin, we are in this together. We are inter-dependent not only with all of humanity but also with the realms of plants and animals and the earth itself. The Kin-dom is the vision of the Divine as the electrifying pull of love that wishes to bring us to wholeness, that wishes us to realize our diversity-celebrating oneness with each other and with all of creation.

---

1 Matthew 4:23

2 McFague, *A New Climate*, 164; Tillich, *Eternal Now*, 121.

The Kin-dom is where wholeness and purpose are finally achieved and we reach the "end" of our journey. Tillich notes that there are two sides to the Kin-dom, "the transcendent and the inner-historical."[1] These are what I will refer to as the mysterious Kin-dom in heaven, or the transcendent Kin-dom, which is often associated with questions of life after physical death, and the elusive Kin-dom on earth, or the inner-historical Kin-dom, which is often associated with a world of love, peace and justice here on this earth.

There is little we can say about the mysterious Kin-dom in heaven with great confidence. It is a mystery because we have no direct experience of it. We truthfully don't know for sure what happens at the "finish," after our deaths. Yet it is an important topic of great interest to many Christians, especially in aging church communities where end of life issues become an increasing concern. As we age, we not only experience more death around us as family and friends die, but we also approach our own deaths. What happens after death becomes a larger concern in our lives as we seek meaning and understanding in the face of our mortality. Reflecting upon the mysterious Kin-dom in heaven is one way we seek that meaning and understanding.

If we in some way transcend our bodily selves, then it seems reasonable to suspect that the death of our physical selves does not necessarily mean the death of our transcendent selves. However, there is little reason to think that the mysterious Kin-dom in heaven is simply a continuation of our time dependent historical existence in a non-physical realm, as is popularly imagined in our visions of heaven and hell.

I would also, along with Tillich, deny that the Kin-dom in heaven coincides with the popular image of it as an escape from hell.[2] The concept of hell itself, as a place of everlasting punishment, seems doubtful if the transcendent self is meant to return to the Divine, which is love. There really doesn't seem to be much reason

1 Paul Tillich, *Systematic Theology, Vol. 3*, (Chicago: The University of Chicago Press, 1976), 394.

2 Tillich, *Eternal Now*, 114.

to believe in such a hell except to satisfy a very human notion of justice as vengeance. Hell is simply a construct used to satisfy the idea that evil people shouldn't be rewarded but must suffer for what they've done wrong. In reality, reincarnation as a theory of what happens to us after death would be more consistent with the claim that the Divine Presence is love itself as reincarnation would offer forgiveness and a second chance to grow into our wholeness.

Of course, the concept of hell has survived because it also has the added benefit that the threat of an eternal hell helps the institutional church to maintain control over its followers. The hypocrisy of such abusive doctrines contribute mightily to the modern day exodus from traditional church power structures. Unfortunately, it is not easy to let go of the idea of hell as a place of everlasting torment. For many Christians the imagery of a fiery hell has been instilled in us from an early age, primarily as a way to scare us into acting "correctly," as an extension of the Santa-for-adults God who instead of gifting a lump of coal for poor behavior sends us to hell to burn forever.

While the Bible talks about hell, it doesn't really offer us a definitive picture. Although a truly exhaustive study of the biblical references to hell is beyond the scope of this book it might be worth offering a few brief comments. The Hebrew Bible talks about sheol as the place of the dead but isn't very clear about what it is supposed to be like. It doesn't seem to necessarily be a place of torment. Job even prays that he be sent to sheol until his earthly ordeals have passed.[1] Sheol doesn't necessarily seem to be a permanent resting place either as the psalmist thanks the Divine Presence for being brought out of sheol and restored to life.[2] Of course, the psalmist is speaking metaphorically. This, I believe is true of most if not all of the Biblical references to an after life, whether they are about heaven or hell, since we cannot truly know what happens to us once our soul departs our physical body.

1 Job 14:13

2 Psalm 30:3

The New Testament uses two Greek words that we translate into English as hell: hades and gehenna. For example, Jesus tells us if our hand causes us to falter we should cut it off and have life rather than go to gehenna with two good hands.[1] He is clearly speaking metaphorically. It is hard to imagine that Jesus is really suggesting we cut off our hands. Further, gehenna literally refers to a valley outside of Jerusalem that was used as a trash dump where fires burned constantly. It is an inherently metaphorical reference. The term hades is also used to quote Jesus in the parable of the rich man and Lazarus.[2] The rich man, who ignores Lazarus' suffering in this life, finds himself tormented in hades upon his death while Lazarus goes to heaven. While the details are quite vivid, they are also clearly metaphorical as that is the very nature of parables.

Of course, metaphors are used to try and tell us something, but I'm not convinced that these metaphors are trying to tell us anything concrete about a place of eternal punishment. Instead, if "heaven" is a place where we are united with the Divine Presence, perhaps "hell" speaks to a separation from the Divine. In this regard the parable of the rich man and Lazarus is quite revealing as the parable talks of a great chasm between heaven and hades which no one can cross. To carry the possibility further, if we in our earthly life are in some way (at least partially) separated from the Divine Presence, perhaps this life on earth could said to be "hell." Certainly, understanding hell as living in a state of separation from the Divine Presence is more consistent with our understanding of the Divine as unconditional love. To be in hell is to be without love. The idea of hell as a place of permanent punishment seems more likely to me to be a perverse human concept we have created to satisfy a warped sense of justice than a literal place created by the Divine Presence. Unconditional love is simply not compatible with eternal torment.

We should not try to bind the mysterious Kin-dom by the morals and rules of our own current state of time-bound mortality.

1 Mark 9:42-48
2 Luke 16:19-31

Whatever our own idealized pictures are of what happens when our physical bodies die, we can't really make assumptions about it based on what we know life to be like for us now. Jesus' reply to the Sadducees who questioned him about resurrection would imply, if nothing else, that the rules and regulations of humanity in our material world and culture cannot be expected to apply in the Kin-dom in heaven.[1] Instead, as manifestations of the Divine, it might make more sense that our transcendent selves, in returning to the Divine, return to eternity, which is "above" time and not a "time *after* time."[2] For Tillich, the mysterious Kin-dom in heaven is not a never ending continuation of history in spiritual form but is "above history"[3] and represents a transition from time based existence to existence which is beyond time, or eternal.[4]

For Tillich, humanity's "participation in eternal life beyond death is more adequately expressed by the highly symbolic phrase 'resurrection of the body.' " This resurrected body is not our physical body but should be imagined as a "spiritual body" as the apostle Paul does.[5] Tillich believed that the spiritual body expresses "the spiritually transformed total personality" of human beings,[6] which is analogous to the transcendent self, the human as manifestation of the Divine.

Patrick Cheng also talks about spiritual bodies, stating that when we "take on" such bodies "at the end of time," our identities as humans, including categorizations such as sexuality and gender,

---

1 Matthew 22:23-33, Mark 12:18-27, and Luke 20:27-38

2 Tillich, *Eternal Now*, 125. This may be a difficult concept because we humans are stuck in time. It is hard to imagine anything "above time." As an analogy, it may be helpful to think of it in terms of a three dimensional being (this is not to say the Divine Presence is a "being") interacting with a two dimensional flat-land. The 3-D being stands outside the 2-D boundaries in a way that the inhabitants of this flat-land wouldn't be able to understand.

3 Tillich, *Systematic Theology, Vol. 3*, 109.

4 Ibid., 395.

5 Ibid., 412.

6 Ibid.

"will no longer matter."[1] The danger in such an assertion is that, if our life on earth is understood to ideally be a reflection of the Kin-dom in heaven, human diversity might be understood as undesirable. This could be used to support abusive doctrines which try to force all people into a model of sameness. On the other hand, to say that something doesn't matter doesn't necessarily mean it doesn't exist. Perhaps those qualities that lead to categorization and judgement in our fleshy lives may still be reflected in a spiritual body but will be cause for celebration instead of marginalization. Indeed, Tillich states that some kind of individual uniqueness remains in the Spiritual body as it returns to the Divine Presence.[2] This makes sense since if multiplicity is a characteristic of the Divine in our finite, fleshy world, then such multiplicity should also be characteristic of the Divine in eternity. Although we return to the Divine Presence, our uniqueness as manifestations of the Divine remains important to the essence of the Divine.

Indeed, even Cheng asserts, somewhat paradoxically, that his claim regarding spiritual bodies "does *not* require that we be completely absorbed into God at the eschaton and that our individual selves cease to exist."[3] While the removal of ways in which we are different is unnecessary and even undesirable, the dissolution of boundaries which separate us is key. Cheng understands the resurrection of the dead as dissolving "the very boundaries between life and death" and states that "if radical love is to triumph in the end, then all barriers that separate us from God will be dissolved."[4] Our return to the Divine Presence in the mysterious Kin-dom of heaven represents the final dissolution of all boundaries between us and the Divine.

While we may assert that our transcendent selves return to the Divine presence upon our physical death, what exactly that means and what it is like is open to speculation more appropriate to "poet-

1 Cheng, *Radical Love*, 131.
2 Tillich, *Systematic Theology, Vol. 3*, 413.
3 Cheng, *Radical Love*, 132.
4 Ibid., 135.

ic and artistic imagination" than any kind of theological certainty.[1] Images of streets lined with gold, choirs of angels, or great family reunions may be comforting in many ways but we can't really know for sure what this spiritual reality is like. In Keller's words, "we simply do not know what configurations of spacing and timing precede and transverse our own: even the physics gapes tantalizingly open."[2] Scientific theories of multiple universes and dimensions as well as some of the more mind-boggling ideas of quantum physics can fuel our imaginations of the possibilities of an ultimate transcendent reality beyond time and space as we currently experience it, but neither science nor theology can, at this time, give us firm answers.

What would it be like not to be bound by space or time? In returning to the Divine Presence, do we become like an energy as we've imagined the Divine to be? If we retain our uniqueness in a spiritual body, will we then recognize family and others we've known in our fleshy lives? The possibilities are fascinating, but it's difficult to imagine what this mysterious Kin-dom in heaven might truly be like. Ultimately, I am not sure there is much that can be said with any certainty about life in the ultimate, mysterious Kin-dom in heaven. Thus, perhaps the best we can proclaim is that the mysterious Kin-dom in heaven represents our return to the love that is the source of our creation. Surely, that is hope and comfort enough. We'll find out the rest when we get there.

We have trust the Divine & live in, and out of Love

Elusive Justice: The Kin-dom on Earth

In the Gospel of Matthew, Jesus teaches his disciples to pray that "Your kingdom come. Your will be done, on earth as it is in heaven."[3] Jesus does not ask us to pray that we be quickly delivered to the Kin-dom in heaven but instead asks that the Kin-dom in heaven be delivered to us here on earth, in this physical life in which we now live. Our life in our current material world matters and, while we may be comforted with the hope of a future complete and

1 Tillich, *Systematic Theology, Vol. 3*, 412.

2 Keller, *Face of the Deep*, 157.

3 Matthew 6:10.

final reunion with our source, we should not neglect to fully live our lives here and now. In the story of the Sadducees mentioned above, Jesus stresses that the Divine Presence is for the living and not of the dead.

However we understand and envision the mysterious Kin-dom in heaven, Jesus, in teaching us how to pray, instructs us that we should seek to emulate it by creating with the Divine Presence the Kin-dom on Earth. Although the Kin-dom in heaven remains mysterious, Jesus does talk about the characteristics of how it would be reflected in the here and now as the elusive Kin-dom on Earth. As a reflection of the Kin-dom in heaven, the earthly Kin-dom must be created out of the source of love which is the Divine Presence and thus becomes a reflection of Divine love. It remains inextricably connected with the Kin-dom in heaven and in exploring what we are called to build in the elusive Kin-dom on Earth we will also learn more about the nature of the mysterious Kin-dom in heaven.

Jesus not only taught us to pray that the Kin-dom be realized on Earth, but proclaiming the Kin-dom was his own primary ministry and message.[1] Jesus spoke frequently about the Kin-dom through various parables, describing more of the ethos of the Kin-dom rather than giving us a concrete description of it or even a prescription of how to achieve it. But, in addition to these clues of the nature of the Kin-dom, I believe the story of the transfiguration is also key to understanding the Kin-dom on Earth.[2]

Jesus tells the disciples, "there are some standing here who will not taste death before they see the Son of Man coming in his kingdom."[3] Then, the story immediately skips ahead to six days later when Jesus and three of his disciples climb a high mountain and experience what we now call the transfiguration. The lack of transition or additional story between these two events could mean that they are intended to be linked together with the transfiguration serving as the fulfillment of Jesus' promise that some of his disciples

1 Mark 1:14-15 and Matthew 4:17
2 Matthew 17:1-8
3 Matthew 16:28

will see the coming of the "Son of Man," or messiah. What the disciples see on that mountain is a glimpse of the Kin-dom. Jesus, as the Divine Presence's anointed one, the messiah, represents the Kin-dom. His message and very being, supported by the prophets and the law represented by Elijah and Moses, who appear with him, are the Kin-dom on Earth. To follow Jesus' teachings is to be about the work of building the Kin-dom on Earth because everything about Jesus has to do with the work of building, living in and renewing the Kin-dom of the Divine Presence on this earth.

When we think of the word transfiguration, it makes us think that Jesus was changed somehow, or transfigured. But that is a misnomer. Jesus wasn't changed, but instead Jesus' true self is revealed as special and extraordinary, blessed by the Divine Presence and firmly grounded in the faith of his ancestors. Through this revelation of Jesus as the promised messiah and the foundation upon which the Kin-dom is built, the Kin-dom itself is revealed in the transfiguration to be first and foremost a state of being one with the Divine Presence.

According to the author Jim Marion, the Aramaic phrase which we translate as "Kingdom of God" means "God's sovereign presence."[1] To be in the Kin-dom is to truly and fully be in the presence of the Divine, standing with Moses and Elijah as symbols of the law and the prophets, as Jesus did. That is, the Kin-dom is a place of the law of the Divine Presence, which in its essence, Jesus teaches us, asks us to love the Divine and to love our neighbor as our selves. The Kin-dom is also a place of the prophets, who stand up for the oppressed and demand justice, and ask that we do likewise. To live in love and justice, with the hope and peace that they create, are what it means to come into the Kin-dom, to be at one with the Divine.

The Kin-dom on Earth is about justice, peace, hope, and love and manifesting those things in our society and in our communi-

---

1 Jim Marion, *Putting on the Mind of Christ: The Inner Work of Christian Spirituality*, (Charlottesville, VA: Hampton Roads Publishing Company, 2008), 8. Scholars believe Aramaic was Jesus' native language.

ties. But it is also about manifesting those qualities within ourselves, deep in our own souls. In addition to seeking justice in our external communities, we must also seek to nurture the qualities of the Kin-dom within ourselves, following the pull of the always present Divine as our guiding force for how we act in the world, the authority to which we turn and the foundation of who we are at our core.

This experience of the Kin-dom, finding unity and harmony in the presence of the Divine Presence, is an experience that might happen on the mountaintop, but it doesn't stay there. Peter offers to build a shelter for Jesus to stay on the mountain, but Jesus ignores him. The Kin-dom of the Divine Presence is not meant to be built in isolation on a mountain. Sometimes, like Peter, we too want to climb to the top of the mountain and stay there. We fear losing the safety and comfort of that mountaintop experience. But, here we must stress the kin-ness of the Kin-dom. We can't hide ourselves away from the rest of humanity and the rest of Creation. We are all interconnected and interdependent. We are all part of a Divinely created family and it is in the world, in the midst of the oppressed and victims of violence, that the Divine Presence wishes to manifest love, justice, hope, and peace through us. It is in the world that Jesus brought the light of the Divine's love and healing and it is here in the nitty gritty of life that the Kin-dom is to be realized. We who wish to be a part of the Kin-dom, to be one with the Divine Presence, must also be in the world, letting the love and compassion of the Divine Presence shine through us as well.

The Kin-dom on Earth that Jesus calls us to create is reminiscent of Martin Luther King Jr.'s vision of the Beloved Community, which is built through a non-violent call for justice. King describes the Beloved Community as a place of justice and non-violence:

> "And so the aftermath of violence is bitterness; the aftermath of non-violence is the creation of the beloved community; the aftermath of non-violence is redemption and reconciliation.

This is a method that seeks to transform and to redeem, and win the friendship of the opponent, and make it possible for [people] to live together as brothers [and sisters] in a community, and not continually live with bitterness and friction."[1]

The Beloved Community is not just the absence of violence, it is also about love. As King describes it:

> "But the end is reconciliation; the end is redemption; the end is the creation of the beloved community. It is this type of spirit and this type of love that can transform opposers into friends.
>
> The type of love that I stress here is not eros, a sort of esthetic or romantic love; not philia, a sort of reciprocal love between personal friends; but it is agape which is understanding goodwill for all [people].
>
> It is an overflowing love which seeks nothing in return. It is the love of God working in the lives of [humanity]. This is the love that may well be the salvation of our civilization."[2]

And it is that Beloved Community, or Kin-dom of God on Earth, that is the goal of Jesus' ministry. It is a community overflowing with a love which seeks nothing in return, a community of non-violent justice and extravagant welcome.

For Sallie McFague, humanity is called "to practice developing a universal love that knows no bounds, a love that becomes more and more inclusive."[3] She asserts that "we must give our whole

1 Martin Luther King, Jr., "Justice Without Violence," 3 April 1957, http://www.thekingcenter.org/archive/document/mlk-justice-without-violence# (accessed 30 May 2016), 6.

2 Martin Luther King, Jr., "The Role of the Church in Facing the Nation's Chief Moral Dilemma," 25 April 1957, http://okra.stanford.edu/transcription/document_images/Vol04Scans/184_1957_The%20Role%20of%20the%20Church.pdf (accessed 30 May 2016), 7.

3 McFague, *A New Climate*, 147.

selves" over to building a better world,[1] the "kingdom of God, where [a] new pattern for living would come about."[2] By choosing to journey in our lives along side Christ we are seeking to fulfill the Divine's desire for us and opening ourselves to experience the elusive Kin-dom on Earth. We become children of love and compassion, transfigured in the dazzling light of the Divine's love and compassion. We become the voices and hands of the Divine Presence in this sacred world, coming into the Kin-dom here and now, working to manifest justice and peace, seeking the hope of the love of the Divine Presence. To glimpse the Kin-dom on Earth is to continue the work of Jesus to build and renew loving, compassionate community. It is to continue the work of building, living in, and renewing the elusive Kin-dom on Earth.

This Kin-dom of justice on Earth toward which we are to work is indeed elusive. According to Catherine Keller, the Kin-dom is a world where the purposes of the Divine Presence are realized and Jesus "saw his work and that of his community as 'foreshadowing' that world — by beginning to actualize it here and now."[3] But, because it is a beginning or foreshadowing, the Kin-dom on Earth is never fully realized. According to Keller it "remains *always* yet to come in history: it is not a literal time-to-come, but an ideal that resists every realized eschatology."[4] The Kin-dom on Earth is an ideal state that resists our attempts to achieve it because it continually exposes our shortcomings and failings. It is an impossible dream in the light of human freedom and yet we are drawn to work toward it because it foreshadows and reflects the mysterious Kin-dom in heaven, the state of wholeness and fulfillment and unity with the Divine Presence which is our ultimate goal.

This elusive Kin-dom on Earth is reflected in the Mission Statement of Phoenix Community Church in its expression of caring community seeking to "support one another during hard times"

1 Ibid., 144.
2 Ibid., 152.
3 Keller, *On the Mystery*, 135.
4 Ibid., 153.

and to "challenge oppression and injustice," including working "for peace and the preservation of the environment."[1] The Mission Statement finishes with a recognition of the elusive nature of the Kin-dom on Earth, stating that "we seek to forgive ourselves and each other when we fail, and to accept the responsibility to begin anew."[2] As human beings who are free to act while living in a state of separation from the Divine Presence, we will fail to fully realize the Kin-dom on Earth. However, according to Tillich, the end of time, of which the Kin-dom is an expression, "is not conceived in terms of a definite moment either in the past or in the future."[3] In a cosmic sense, beginnings and endings, creation and eschaton, birth and death, are not specific points in time but are ongoing processes always occurring in every moment. When we reach an ending, we can only forgive and begin again to create something new, to rise out of the ashes once more.

McFague states that the Kin-dom on Earth is possible to imagine "because God is before us; God is there already."[4] That is, trust in the reality of the mysterious Kin-dom in heaven, where love resides and rules, allows us to envision the possibility of the Kin-dom on Earth. It allows us to envision the communities of "just love,"[5] for which Keller calls. It allows us to envision a world where humans live out of the Divine love that incarnates us, living out of values such as justice, peace, and compassion. It allows us to envision a world where we care for and nurture creation instead of use and waste it like a disposable commodity. It allows us to envision a world where diversity is appreciated and welcomed, where the multiplicity of the Divine Presence is recognized and cherished. It allows us to envision a world where hope abounds and people do not live in such despair that they strike out in violence against their neighbors, but instead reach out in love.

---

1 "Our Mission Statement"

2 Ibid.

3 Tillich, *Systematic Theology, Vol. 3*, 420.

4 McFague, *A New Climate*, 151.

5 Keller, *God and Power*, 111.

Chapter 7 Discussion Questions

1. What do you think happens after we die? Why?
2. Do you believe in hell? Why or why not?
3. To what is God calling us here on this earth? In other words, how would you describe the Divine's Kin-dom on earth?
4. What are some practical steps we can take as church communities to create the Divine's Kin-dom on earth? What can we do as individuals?

8 Loving Our Neighbor

Thoughts on Ministry

Doing the work of the Divine: Co-creating the Kin-dom

The prophet Micah states what is required of those who follow the Divine Presence: "He has told you, O mortal, what is good; and what does the Lord require of you but to do justice, and to love kindness, and to walk humbly with your God?"[1] As followers of the Divine Presence we are to create a just and fair world, treat others kindly and with love, and we are to do these things in relationship with the Divine Presence, acting as the Divine's loving eyes, ears, and hands in this world. One way we can do this is through co-creating communities of justice and love with the Divine Presence. This is what the church is meant to be.

Patrick Cheng notes that, for early Christians, coming together in community was "a rehearsal for the end times."[2] Christian community, the church, was thus meant to be a foreshadowing of the elusive Kin-dom on earth, which is marked by justice, peace, and compassion. For Paul Tillich, the church as "the Spiritual Community is the community of faith and love."[3] Churches are communities where Christians strive to enact life as the Divine Presence meant it to be. They are communities of "radical love."[4]

Ministry, or doing the work of the Divine, is the building of the Kin-dom and is necessarily done in community. The church is the banding together of the faithful for mutual support and en-

1 Micah 6:8

2 Cheng, *Radical Love*, 106.

3 Tillich, *Systematic Theology, Vol. 3*, 172.

4 Cheng, *Radical Love*, 106.

couragement. Lillian Daniel proposes that "Practicing our faith is like dance. ... We are called to dance together."[1] Ministry is done together. We do ministry as the church community and not to the community or for the community. We dance our faith with each other and not as a performance for one another.

At its ideal, the church witnesses to the world of the love of the Divine Presence and what it means to live in the Kin-dom. Authors Gregory Jones and Kevin Armstrong claim that as Christians "we are called to cultivate a common life marked by the 'mind of Christ'."[2] That is, we are called to gather as Christ's church, living together according to the values of the Kin-dom, as examples of the Kin-dom for the world. We are called to live together in hope, love, peace, and justice.

Of course, the church often fails to live by these values, sometimes in small ways and sometimes on a grand scale. Our failings expose our humanity and imperfection, often alienating and driving away those who seek the true Kin-dom, who see the church's hypocrisy when it fails to recognize or acknowledge its failures. But our propensity for failure doesn't change the call from the Divine Presence to build the Kin-dom. Instead, what it means is that we need to better learn the humility needed to admit our mistakes, to forgive ourselves and others who have hurt us, and to begin again. This is the Christian principle of resurrection. The promise of the Divine Presence is that new life can and will arise from death, that we can rise from the ashes of our failures to find new and abundant life.

To be truly alive requires that church communities practice "the amorous justice"[3] of the Kin-dom of the Divine Presence,

1 Lillian Daniel, "Minute 54" in *This Odd and Wondrous Calling: The Public and Private Lives of Two Ministers*, Lillian Daniel and Martin B. Copenhaver, 1-7 (Grand Rapids, MI: William B. Eerdmans Publishing Company, 2009), 3.

2 L. Gregory Jones and Kevin R. Armstrong, *Resurrecting Excellence: Shaping Faithful Christian Ministry*, (Grand Rapids, MI: Wm. B. Eerdmans Publishing Co., 2006), 17.

3 Keller, *On the Mystery*, 154.

according to Catherine Keller. That the justice of the Kin-dom is to be "amorous" would seem to be a reflection of Jesus' commandment to love the Divine Presence and to love one's neighbor as one's self. Both Jesus and the apostle Paul claim that "all the law and the prophets" are based on this command to love.[1] All we do as Christians should be based on these principles of love. It follows, then, that the first and foremost thing with which ministry should be concerned is loving the Divine Presence, loving neighbor and loving self.

When Jesus washes the feet of his disciples, he gives us an example of service to those around him and tells his disciples to do likewise, reinforcing this with the command that they love one another.[2] By their love will they be known. It's important to realize the connection between Jesus washing the feet of the disciples and his command to love one another. This command is about a new way of relating to those around us. It goes against the grain of our American cowboy culture of brave independence. Instead, it is grounded in Jesus' relationship with the disciples and with the Divine and is shaped by the example he sets for us: teaching, healing, and being a servant to all of the Divine's beloved children. He sets for us a pattern of service, of humility and of bearing the burdens of one another.

To love someone in the sense that Jesus is talking about is not necessarily to like them, to be their BFF, their best friend forever. It's not an emotional thing, but loving someone as Jesus commands us to do means realizing and always remembering that they are a beloved child of the Divine Presence and that they are worthy of compassion and respect. This kind of love is an active love, a compassionate love, a being-with love. It means to rejoice with each other in times of good fortune and support each other in our times of difficulty. It means being servants to one another. To love one another is more about doing than it is about feeling. The feeling

1 Matthew 22:34-40. For Paul see Romans 13:8-10 and Galatians 5:14.

2 John 13:1-17 and John 13:31-35

part of love comes after the doing, in growing closer in our relationships and in keeping the Divine at the center of those relationships.

While the church builds the Kin-dom within itself, it also strives to build the Kin-dom in all of Creation through practicing love and advocating for justice. The command to love forms the basis for how Phoenix Community Church understands its mission to build the Kin-dom in the world. Phoenix states that its purpose is to embody the love of the Divine Presence as revealed by Jesus. To embody the love of the Divine is to practice the Divine's presence, which according to Sallie McFague "means to embrace what God embraces: life and love."[1] Importantly, this embodiment, this embracing life and love, takes place, for Phoenix Community Church, in relationship with "each other, our neighbors, and all creation."[2] Love is something that can only be practiced and realized within relationship.

Building relationships with the world, which allow the Divine's love to shine through us, will work to transform the world into the Kin-dom. For this to happen, we must be a part of the world and take an active role in its care. For McFague, "loving God means feeding the suffering body of the world."[3] That is, to love the Divine Presence, is to also love the neighbor, to take special care to see the Christ in the "other," those who are not like us. It requires that we love and respect our neighbor by embracing the stranger and the marginalized as Jesus did, offering them the love of the Divine Presence as we work with them to make the world fair and just.

Responding to the Divine: Church and Worship

While the church and Christians in general are called to care for and seek justice in the world as their ministry, the church is also more than a beneficent social organization. Tillich states his belief that a church which is nothing more than a "benevolent, socially

1 McFague, *A New Climate*, 172.

2 "Our Purpose Statement"

3 McFague, *A New Climate*, 115.

useful group," with no real distinction from similar secular groups, does not justify its existence.[1] What distinguishes the church is that it not only seeks to do good in the world but does so in response to its relationship with the Divine Presence. In the terms of Jesus' Great Commandment, it is not only imperative that we love our neighbor, but that we also love the Divine Presence.

If we are taking seriously the claim that the Divine Presence is love, then we cannot truly love our neighbor outside of a relationship with the Divine Presence. As we are all manifestations of the Divine, fostering relationships with each other and with Creation are critical. The building of these relationships brings us to healing through union with the Divine by uniting the Spirit within each of us, much like many small fires brought together might form a large bonfire. Thus, a key part of ministry is to nurture the relationship with the Divine, particularly through worship.

According to Tillich, worship is one way we respond to the Divine Presence, paradoxically participating in, or communing with, the Divine Presence to which we belong even though we remain separated from it.[2] The purposeful spending of time in the presence of the Divine as a community in worship also allows us to better serve the world at large. I've heard it said that we might think of attending worship as working on our spiritual health much like going to the gym helps get and stay healthy physically. In coming together as a worshiping body, we practice what it means to be the Kin-dom and better prepare ourselves to build the Kin-dom in a world that promotes selfishness over justice and the hoarding of wealth over compassionate sharing.

There are three things that I hope we find every time we gather together to worship the Divine Presence.[3] The first is, of course, the presence of the Divine. Worship should connect us with the Divine, that we might know that our pleas and concerns are heard,

---

1 Tillich, *Systematic Theology, Vol. 3*, 166.

2 Ibid., 190.

3 I first heard these three goals of worship articulated at a worship workshop which I attended, held on April 9, 2005 by the Rev. Janice Springer.

that the Divine shares our joys as well as our tears, and also that we might hear the Divine Presence's desires and guiding voice for us.

The second hope is that we find community when we come to worship. Community is not about having fun with friends. It is so much more. Community is about supporting one another, loving one another, and even challenging one another. Community is about realizing our interdependence, not just with those in the church but with those outside the church walls as well.

The third hope for worship is that we find the Gospel, the good news of the Divine's love. We should leave every service of worship having heard in some form that the Divine Presence loves us unconditionally. When the Bible tells us Jesus went to the synagogue he went there to teach, to proclaim the good news, and to heal the people.[1] Worship should be a place of healing where, if we are feeling broken by the world, hearing the Good News of the Divine's love can begin to mend us and make us whole once again.

When worship meets these three aims, it affirms and fosters not only one's personal relationship with the Divine Presence, but our relationships with each other. When we worship by opening ourselves to the Divine's presence, fostering true community, and experiencing the good news of the Divine Presence's love, I believe we are watering our souls that they may grow into the loved and loving Creations that we are intended to be. We are planting the seeds of transformation for not only ourselves but for the world, for what we experience in worship we are meant to carry with us into the world.

Jesus said in the gospel of John that "true worshipers will worship the Father in spirit and truth."[2] It doesn't matter whether our worship service is formal or informal, whether we sit in pews or in a circle, whether we have organ music or a modern band. What is important in how we worship is that we worship in spirit and in truth; that we worship not only with our heads but also with our hearts. Beliefs and doctrines that are expressed in worship need to

1 Matthew 4:23 and Matthew 9:35

2 John 4:23

be intellectually sound but the message of the Divine's love also needs to go deeper than our minds. Worship needs to enter our hearts and the deepest parts of our souls because that is where transformation takes place. That transformation, that changing of our hearts through deep relationship with the Divine Presence, is ultimately what worship is about.

With transformed hearts we can carry the Divine's love from the place of worship into the rest of our lives. If worship only affects us for an hour on Sunday, then it's useless. In worship we are meant to model and practice as a church the principles and characteristics of the Divine's Kin-dom: loving our neighbor, caring for the poor, and treating all justly with the respect they deserve as the Divine Presence's beloved Creations. If the relevance of the church, of our worship, is measured by how it connects us to the Divine Presence, then it is also measured by our actions in the world.

While the church builds the Kin-dom within itself, it also strives to build the Kin-dom in all of Creation through the practice of loving compassion and advocating for justice. Love is something that can only be practiced and realized within relationship. Building relationships with the world, which allow the Divine's love to shine through us, will work to transform the world into the Kin-dom. For this to happen, we must be a part of the world and take an active role in its care.

The many aspects of a traditional protestant worship service all contribute to the meaningfulness of the worship experience. These include music, readings, the sermon and spiritual practices such as confession, offering, prayer and sacraments. Each of these convey certain messages and energy, or spirit, to the worshipers and can affect the worship experience in either a positive or negative fashion. Phoenix Community Church has typically tried to foster an intimate, healing worship experience that allows for the building of relationship both with each other and the Divine Presence. For example, worshiping in a circle creates a more intimate relationship between worshipers. Trying to make sure all aspects of the service are connected by theme helps worshipers relax and open their hearts as well as participating with their minds. Prayer has also always been an important part of the worship experience and Phoenix maintains an opportunity of open, personal sharing as part of its tradition of prayer to allow us to better connect with each other and the Divine.

Practicing the Kin-dom in Worship: Prayer

Theologian Paul Tillich asserts that prayer is a major component of worship.[1] Along with Tillich, Marjorie Hewitt Suchocki also believes that prayer goes deeper than the words we might say while praying and is a meeting of the Spirit within us with the Spirit of the Divine Presence.[2] Prayer is in many ways, as Catherine Keller claims, a strategy "for intimacy with the infinite."[3] It is a sacred moment spent connecting with the Divine, both talking and listening to the call of the electrifying pull of love.

Understanding the Divine Presence as the call of love on our lives pulling us toward our wholeness, rather than an all-controlling force, means that we have the power and freedom to make our own choices. In a sense, we co-create the future with the Divine Presence. Of all the possible life choices we can make, the Divine invites us along a certain path but we decide what choice we make and based on that choice the Divine Presence invites us to the next step and so on and so on. The idea reminds me of following a GPS[4] in a car. The GPS tells us where to go but if we don't follow its suggestion, it recalculates and gives us a new route to follow. In this relational understanding of the Divine Presence, prayer becomes perhaps more important than ever because we are partners with the Divine and not pawns or subjects.

Prayer, then, is not a way of trying to manipulate an all powerful supernatural being into doing what we want.[5] Prayer becomes

1 Tillich, *Systematic Theology, Vol. 3*, 190.
2 Suchocki, 39-40; Tillich, *Systematic Theology, Vol. 3*, 191-192.
3 Keller, *On the Mystery*, 23.
4 Global positioning system
5 Suchocki, 65.

instead a way of opening ourselves to the will and calling of the Divine Presence. Prayer becomes how we connect and align our hearts, our intentions, with the Divine Presence that fills our universe. The Divine Presence connects with us at the most basic level of our existence and prayer is the way we become aware of it, the way we hear its calling.[1] Prayer is the way we open ourselves to Divine creative energy and to the good that the Divine Presence intends for us.[2] At the same time, prayer is also about letting the Divine Presence know what we think. Prayer becomes a two way discussion, a way of working through our life choices in partnership with the Divine Presence. Prayer becomes a way of sharing ourselves — a way of processing the past, living in the present and planning for the future.

Our prayers actually make a difference in what the Divine Presence can accomplish. Suchocki considers prayer "central to the *how* of God's continuing work in our world."[3] The Divine works with the world as it is but our prayer changes the state of the world.[4] By opening ourselves to the Divine and putting out our intentions and thus our willingness to be part of the answer to our prayers, we create new possibilities that the Divine Presence can work with. For example, praying for another's well-being allows the Divine to weave us into the answer to that prayer.[5] Stating our desire, our intention, for someone's healing tells the Divine that we're willing to be part of the solution. In a world such as ours where we are so interdependent, where relationship is so important to our lives and happiness, the Divine Presence may very well use us in answer to our prayers.[6] Our willingness creates more possibilities with which to work.

Of course, one of the difficulties we all struggle with in prayer is what happens when what we want to be created out of our prayer

1 Ibid., 26.
2 Ibid., 28.
3 Ibid., 126.
4 Ibid., 49.
5 Ibid., 47.
6 Ibid., 50.

doesn't happen. I try to remember that prayer is about possibility and not all things might be possible or might not be in our best interests. The Divine Presence, after all, has a broad eternal view that we lack as time-bound physical beings. In the context of illness, especially terminal illness, to pray for one's health is to pray for the health that is possible whether that be total recovery, partial recover or the recovery of those who mourn.[1]

Prayer can be powerful. I believe prayer can open up possibilities that didn't seem to be there before. And sometimes those possibilities look miraculous to us. Maybe a physical healing occurs that the doctors didn't think could happen. But sometimes what is possible may not be physical health. It may be spiritual or emotional health instead. The Divine Presence works with the possibilities. And we help create more possibility through prayer and through offering ourselves as we follow the Divine's loving pull.

So, how do we pray? How do we go about creating those possibilities? Prayer is both talking and listening to the Divine Presence. But prayer also takes many forms. Talking to the Divine might be actual talking like we normally associate with prayer. But we might also talk through our actions. We can pray through what we do and how we treat people. That communicates something to the Divine Presence. Or we might pray through ritual as well. Taking communion, for example, is saying something to the Divine. It's another way of opening ourselves to the Divine Presence.

Furthermore, prayer is not only talking to the Divine Presence, but it also involves listening for what the Divine might be saying to us. Too often, we are so busy in our modern lives rushing to work, rushing to get the next project done, rushing to see what messages await us on our smart phones that we forget to stop and look and listen. I wonder how many holy moments we miss, how many potential conversations with the Divine Presence just fly by without us noticing. In the Bible, Jesus models for us that we need to take the time to stop and pay attention. He is often trying to get away from the crowds and those demanding his time in

1 Ibid., 64.

order to pray and connect with the Divine Presence. Listening to the Divine might be a time of quiet, perhaps trying to empty our minds and making space for the Holy to enter. Or listening might take the form of meditation, or reading scripture or in observing and reflecting on life around us. Since the Divine Presence can be found anywhere, it makes sense that the Divine Presence can be heard anywhere as well.

Every aspect of our life might be looked upon as prayer because everything we think and do could be understood as communicating to the Divine Presence and the world our desires and our willingness to be. Much of this is done subconsciously, but prayer is probably most effective when it happens with conscious intent on our part and this is why we set aside prayer as a special action. But in doing so we also sometimes get too caught up in *how* we are supposed to pray.

There are many things that I think don't matter that much when it comes to prayer. Perhaps the form of prayer is one of those. I don't think it matters if you pray out loud or silently. I don't think it matters if words come haltingly or flow eloquently. We don't need to worry very much about whether we are praying "correctly" because there really is no correct way to pray. If we're not sure how to pray then it can be perfectly fine to just sit in silence, trying to open ourselves to the Divine Presence in and around us. Prayers can also be kept simple. Often "thank you" or "help" is a perfectly suitable way to pray. We might also pray a familiar prayer such as the prayer that Jesus taught the disciples, traditionally known as the "Lord's Prayer."[1]

However, there are some things about how we pray that I think are important. One of those is authenticity. Being true to ourselves,

---

1 The form of this well known, traditional prayer used at Phoenix Community Church has been adjusted to use inclusive language: Our Mother - Father who art in heaven, hallowed be Thy names. Thy kin-dom come. Thy will be done, on earth as it is in heaven. Give us this day our daily bread. And forgive us our trespasses, as we forgive those who trespass against us. And lead us not into temptation, but deliver us from evil. For Thine is the kin-dom, and the power, and the glory, forever. Amen.

being authentic and praying from the heart is probably the most important thing about prayer. Praying can be treated much like talking to a dear friend whom you love deeply. It should be open and honest. If the Divine Presence is part of us, if the Spirit within knows what lies deep in our hearts, then what point is there in ever pretending we are something that we are not when we bring ourselves before the Divine in an act of prayer?[1] As Jesus tells us, prayer is between us and the Divine Presence, it is not a show for others.[2] We don't need to entertain with our prayers. Prayer isn't a game where the best and most eloquent one wins. We are all equal and equally loved when we come before the Divine Presence. We don't need to impress anyone by rattling on and on.

Prayer is about creating possibilities by sharing our desires and intentions with the Divine and listening for the Divine's call on us. Because intention matters we might be attentive as well to stating our desires in positive ways. This can be particularly important when praying in a public context. For example, when praying for a loved one's health, the intention we want to put forth to the Divine is a picture of that person fully healed. Prayerfully reciting a long list of the person's medical troubles might in some ways be counter productive as it instead keeps us picturing the person as sick. Such negative prayers could affect the way we feel toward the situation and thus limit rather than increase the possibilities of healing. When prayed in public, that negative picture is shared with others and thus compounded. Of course, this doesn't mean all of our prayers have to be rosy, either. Often we have to acknowledge our pain before we can heal from it and the Divine can handle a little ranting on our part when it is necessary, but it can be worthwhile to also think about the energy and intentions we are really putting before the Divine.

Putting demands on the Divine Presence can also limit the possibilities of the Divine's response to the prayer, or at least our perceptions of that response. For example, if one is in need of a new

1 Suchocki, 37.

2 Matthew 6:5-8

car, praying for your dream car is much different than praying for a solution to your transportation problem. The latter opens us to more possibilities than the former. I think persistence in prayer also opens up more possibility by keeping our desires and intentions in our consciousness and therefore continually opening our hearts to the leading of the Divine Presence.

The Divine's touch upon us, the Divine energy that flows through us, calls us to the Divine Presence's path of love. The Divine's call is an insistent whisper that we live responsibly and lovingly in the world,[1] that we be compassionate co-creators and partners with the Divine Presence as we walk this journey. Opening ourselves in prayer to the Divine Presence can be a first step to following on that path boldly, opening ourselves to a wonderful world of new possibilities.

Practicing the Kin-dom in Worship: Sacraments

In addition to prayer, sacraments are another way we open ourselves to and build relationship with the Divine Presence. Cheng notes that the traditional Christian understanding is that a sacrament is "a visible sign of God's invisible grace."[2] That is, sacraments are understood to make visible the presence of the Divine. In doing so, the sacraments bring us closer to "our eschatological destiny," according to Cheng,[3] and therefore work to dissolve the boundaries that separate us, providing us with a "foretaste of the radical love to come."[4] We might say that a sacrament is a ritual that creates a "thin place" where human and divine more easily meet. Sacraments are holy times that are used by God to work within us, to heal us, to call us forth, and to remind us we are loved. By bringing us closer to wholeness, or reunion with the Divine Presence, the sacraments give us an inkling of what that wholeness is like. In practical terms, Christians sometimes have different under-

1 Suchocki, 123.

2 Cheng, *Radical Love*, 120.

3 Ibid.

4 Ibid., 129.

standings of which of our practices are sacraments. Most Christian denominations, however, recognize at least the two sacraments of baptism and communion.

When one asks what baptism means, we might find many answers. Historically, Christians have been too worried about being "correct" about baptism. Issues about how to do it (sprinkling vs. immersion) and who is eligible (babies or adults) have sometimes split the church. Whatever our churches officially say about baptism or whatever we personally believe about it, we shouldn't dismiss the mystery and possibility of the sacrament. We shouldn't get caught up in who's right and who's wrong. To do so is to put restrictions on the Divine Presence, to try to limit how, where, and with whom the Divine can work.

In part, baptism is an initiation of belonging. Baptism marks us as the Divine's, as a part of the body of Christ. It says we are a child of the Divine Presence, we are beloved, and that can never be taken away from us. It is a public affirmation of the Divine Presence's promise that we are always loved unconditionally. If we are baptized as an adult, we also promise to live our life as a disciple of the Divine's Way. If we are baptized as an infant, then the promise to the Divine Presence is made by our parents or guardians and usually affirmed by us during a time of confirmation later in our lives.

In addition to being a rite of initiation baptism can also be understood as a rite of transformation. Baptism is not only about who we are and whose we are, it also creates that thin place in our life where we meet the divine in a special way. It is an invitation for the Holy Spirit to descend upon us and not only confirm that we are the Divine Presence's beloved, but to begin the work of transformation within our lives. In baptism, and perhaps especially obvious and meaningful in adult baptism, one leaves one's old life behind to begin a new life in Christ. In this way, baptism draws the new Christian closer to union with the Divine and gives them insight into the nature of the Kin-dom of the Divine Presence. As McFague says, the sacramental "connects the earthly" with the

Divine Presence,[1] showing us the "continuity" between the Divine and the world.[2] Once opened to the work of the Holy Spirit, we should expect to be transformed as we follow Jesus' footsteps along a path of hope, peace, love, and justice.

In communion we take into ourselves the essence of Jesus, the living bread. We take into ourselves the Divine Presence's love incarnate in order to fully engage and enjoy this divine love and its transforming powers. We are what we eat. If understood as the taking-in of the body of Christ, or the Kin-dom, into one's own being, communion brings us closer to that Kin-dom and union with the Divine Presence. It's an act of reconciliation, drawing us closer to the Divine and bringing us new life. By acting in these ways, the sacraments are, as Tillich notes, a method of communication between the human and the Divine Presence.[3] They are communication which, like prayer, goes beyond the mere words involved in order to create relationship between human beings and the Divine.

As a sacramental ritual, communion is also a reminder of how we are to be in the world. Breaking bread together, while declaring all are welcome with no preconditions, is practice for how we are to live outside of the church walls and how we are to interact both within and outside our Christian communities. By asking us to remember Christ, the face of the other, communion asks us to remember how we are to be in the world.

However else we might remember Christ in communion, we can allow the bread and wine to remind us of Jesus as a real fleshy human who ate and drank with gusto. It can remind us of the Jesus who lived as a gift to us that we might truly encounter the Divine in our own lives. Remembering Jesus this way, we can remember the Christ that is present in the others in our lives, those who are in need of our love and compassion. Just as we can find Christ in the face of the other, we can find the other in Christ. Just as we

---

1 McFague, *A New Climate*, 133.

2 Ibid., 110.

3 Tillich, *Systematic Theology, Vol. 3*, 120.

see the bread and wine as a reminder of Christ, we can see it as a reminder of the marginalized and outcast who we are called to love.

Through the breaking of the bread, we remember Jesus and through Jesus we remember the Divine in the other, the stranger, and in all those we encounter. In doing so, we practice finding the Divine in others, in being more compassionate to all those that cross our path and even to those we may never meet personally, for we are all connected in this global community we live in today. By strengthening our bond with the other, the marginalized and oppressed, we also push at the cultural boundaries that seek to control people and "keep them in their place" and help create an ethos of love, justice, sharing, and inter-dependence — a foreshadowing of the Kin-dom that we can carry into all of our interactions.

Called by the Divine: Ministry

Celebration of the sacraments are often done under the auspices of an authorized minister. The World Council of Churches says that "the chief responsibility of the ordained ministry is to assemble and build up the body of Christ by proclaiming and teaching the Word of God, by celebrating the sacraments, and by guiding the life of the community in its worship, its mission and its caring ministry."[1] Ordained ministers, then, are people who are called by the Divine Presence and by the church to fulfill special leadership roles of nurture and support.

Taking into account each person's unique gifts, the role of a minister may certainly differ from person to person, especially if we consider it a function of fulfilling one's personal calling and being true to one's Divinely created being. The apostle Paul notes that the church is one body with "many members, and not all the members have the same function" but "we have gifts that differ according to the grace given to us."[2] Lillian Daniel compares ministry to playing in a band: "it's not just about playing alone. The notes and sounds

1 "Baptism, Eucharist and Ministry," *Faith and Order Paper No. 11*, World Council of Churches (Geneva, 1982), 18-19.

2 Romans 12:4,6.

come together, the different people play their roles, and what is produced transcends the individual parts."[1]

Among Christian churches, the process by which ministers are chosen, authorized or ordained can vary widely. In the context of my own protestant denomination, the minister is authorized both by the local congregation and the appropriate body of the denomination as they, together with the minister, attempt to discern the Divine's calling. The minister's specific role is defined in a covenant between the church and minister, typically including preaching and leading worship, pastoral care, and general leadership and administrative functions. However, the same covenant also talks about the responsibilities of the church community.

The minister doesn't work alone but does ministry in concert with the rest of the congregation where all church members are understood to be ministers who support and nurture each other and those outside the church community. In this relationship, the ordained minister is a guide and a resource, not doing ministry for the church, but empowering the church to do its ministry and follow the call of the Divine Presence for its communal life. It's also the role of an ordained minister to not only be in partnership with and nurture the local congregation but also to be accountable to the Divine and a visible representative of the Good News of Divine's love in the church and in the wider community.

We come together in the church, in the Body of Christ, to nurture our relationships with each other, creation, and the Divine Presence through worship, prayer, and sacrament. By responding in this way to the electrifying pull of love which is the Divine Presence, we prepare ourselves to minister to the world through the church as co-creators of the Divine Presence's Kin-dom on earth. Living as part of this Kin-dom is to live out of the Divine within each of us, which is revealed through Jesus the Christ. It is to live

---

1 Lillian Daniel, "I'm with the Band" in *This Odd and Wondrous Calling: The Public and Private Lives of Two Ministers*, Lillian Daniel and Martin B. Copenhaver, 51-57 (Grand Rapids, MI: William B. Eerdmans Publishing Company, 2009), 57.

out of the knowledge of our deep, fundamental oneness with the Divine and all creation. It is to live out of love and with values of peace, hope, and justice. It is to live in community without unnecessary boundaries, welcoming all.

Chapter 8 Discussion Questions

1. What is the purpose of the church?
2. How does communal worship benefit your life? If you don't attend worship services regularly, why not?
3. What ways of talking and listening to the Divine Presence (i.e. prayer) do you find most meaningful?
4. Have you ever experienced a time in prayer that seemed particularly powerful? Have you ever felt the Divine wasn't listening when you prayed? What do you think was the difference, if any?
5. What do baptism and/or communion mean to you?
6. Besides baptism and communion are there other rituals that you think of as sacraments, that create a "thin place" where you more easily experience the Divine?
7. What is the role of an ordained minister? In what ways do non-clergy members of the church also perform the roles of a minister?

Why do we pray?

Bibliography

Arthur, Kenneth. *The Queer Christ: Recognizing Ourselves in the Divine*. Chicago: Chicago Theological Seminary, Master of Arts thesis, 2009.

"Baptism, Eucharist and Ministry." *Faith and Order Paper No. 11*. World Council of Churches (Geneva, 1982).

Borg, Marcus J. and John Dominic Crossan. *The Last Week: What the Gospels Really Teach About Jesus' Final Days in Jerusalem*. San Francisco: HarperCollins, 2007.

"Catechism of the Catholic Church." http://www.vatican.va/archive/ccc_css/archive/catechism/p3s2c2a6.htm (accessed 30 May 2016).

Cheng, Patrick. *From Sin to Amazing Grace: Discovering the Queer Christ*. New York: Seabury Books, 2012.

Cheng, Patrick. *Radical Love: An Introduction to Queer Theology*. New York: Seabury Books, 2011.

Cheng, Patrick. *Rainbow Theology: Bridging Race, Sexuality, and Spirit*. New York: Seabury Books, 2013.

Daly, Mary. *Beyond God the Father: Toward a Philosophy of Women's Liberation*. Boston: Beacon Press, 1985.

Daniel, Lillian. "I'm with the Band." In *This Odd and Wondrous Calling: The Public and Private Lives of Two Ministers*, Lillian Daniel and Martin B. Copenhaver, 51-57 Grand Rapids, MI: William B. Eerdmans Publishing Company, 2009.

Daniel, Lillian. "Minute 54." In *This Odd and Wondrous Calling: The Public and Private Lives of Two Ministers*, Lillian Daniel and Martin B. Copenhaver, 1-7. Grand Rapids, MI: William B. Eerdmans Publishing Company, 2009.

Douglas, Mary. *Purity and Danger*. London and New York: Routledge Classics, 2002.

Evans, James H., Jr. *We Have Been Believers: An African American Systematic Theology*. 2nd ed. Minneapolis: Fortress Press, 2012.

Frankl, Viktor E. *The Doctor and The Soul.* Translated by Richard and Clara Winston. New York: Alfred A. Knopf Inc., 1969.

Frankl, Viktor E. *Man's Search For Ultimate Meaning*. Cambridge, MA: Perseus Publishing, 2000.

Freke, Timothy and Peter Gandy. *Jesus and the Lost Goddess: The Secret Teachings of the Original Christians.* New York: Harmony Books, 2001.

Goss, Robert E. "John." In *The Queer Bible Commentary*, edited by Deryn Guest, Robert E. Goss, Mona West, and Thomas Bohache, 548-565. London: SCM Press, 2006.

Gunderson, Gary and Lawrence Pray. *Leading Causes of Life: Five Fundamentals to Change the Way You Live Your Life*. Nashville, TN: Abingdon Press, 2009.

Hardt, Michael and Negri, Antonio. *Multitude: War and Democracy in the Age of Empire*. New York: Penguin Books, 2004.

"Inclusive Language." http://www.phoenixchurch.org/inclusive.php (accessed 30 May 2016).

Jones, L. Gregory and Kevin R. Armstrong. *Resurrecting Excellence: Shaping Faithful Christian Ministry*. Grand Rapids, MI: Wm. B. Eerdmans Publishing Co., 2006.

Keller, Catherine. *Face of the Deep: A Theology of Becoming*. London and New York: Routledge, 2003.

Keller, Catherine. *God and Power: Counter-Apocalyptic Journeys.* Minneapolis: Fortress Press, 2005.

Keller, Catherine. *On the Mystery: Discerning Divinity in Process.* Minneapolis: Fortress Press, 2008.

King, Jr., Martin Luther. "Justice Without Violence." 3 April 1957. http://www.thekingcenter.org/archive/document/mlk-justice-without-violence# (accessed 30 May 2016).

King, Jr., Martin Luther. "The Role of the Church in Facing the Nation's Chief Moral Dilemma." 25 April 1957. http://okra.stanford.edu/transcription/document_images/Vol04Scans/184_1957_The%20Role%20of%20the%20Church.pdf (accessed 30 May 2016).

Lee, Felicia R. "From Noah's Curse to Slavery's Rationale." *The New York Times*, 1 November, 2003. http://www.nytimes.com/2003/11/01/arts/from-noah-s-curse-to-slavery-s-rationale.html (accessed 8 January, 2016).

Lewis, Karoline. "True Resurrection." http://www.workingpreacher.org/craft.aspx?post=4571 (accessed 30 May 2016).

Marion, Jim. *Putting on the Mind of Christ: The Inner Work of Christian Spirituality*. Charlottesville, VA: Hampton Roads Publishing Company, 2000.

McFague, Sallie. *Models of God: Theology for an Ecological, Nuclear Age*. Philadelphia: Fortress Press, 1987.

McFague, Sallie. *A New Climate For Theology: God, the World, and Global Warming*. Minneapolis: Fortress Press, 2008.

Moltmann, Jürgen. *The Politics of Discipleship and Discipleship in Politics*, edited by Willard M. Swartley. Eugene, OR: Wipf & Stock Publishers, 2006.

Morrison, Melanie. "How We Believe at Phoenix Community Church, UCC." Kalamazoo, MI: Phoenix Community Church archives, 1989.

"Our Core Values & Beliefs." http://www.phoenixchurch.org/beliefs.php (accessed 30 May 2016).

"Our Mission Statement." http://www.phoenixchurch.org/mission.php (accessed 30 May 2016).

"Our Purpose Statement." http://www.phoenixchurch.org/mission.php (accessed 30 May 2016).

"Preamble to the Constitution of the United Church of Christ." http://www.ucc.org/beliefs/preamble-to-the-constitution.html (accessed 27 November 2013).

Rumi, Maulana Jalal al-Din. *The Essential Rumi.* Translated by Coleman Barks. San Francisco: HarperCollins Publishers, 1995.

Schneider, Laurel. *Beyond Monotheism: A Theology of Multiplicity.* London and New York: Routledge, 2008.

Söelle, Dorothee. *Thinking About God: An Introduction to Theology.* Translated by John Bowden. Harrisburg, PA: Trinity Press International, 1990.

Suchocki, Marjorie Hewitt. *God's Presence: Theological Reflections on Prayer.* St. Louis, Missouri: Chalice Press, 1996.

Terrell, JoAnne Marie. *Power in the Blood? The Cross in the African American Experience.* Eugene, Oregon: Wipf & Stock Publishers, 2005.

Tillich, Paul. *The Eternal Now.* New York: Charles Scribner's Sons, 1963.

Tillich, Paul. *Systematic Theology.* Vol. 1. Chicago: The University of Chicago Press, 1973.

Tillich, Paul. *Systematic Theology.* Vol. 2. Chicago: The University of Chicago Press, 1975.

Tillich, Paul. *Systematic Theology.* Vol. 3. Chicago: The University of Chicago Press, 1976.

West, Cornel. *Democracy Matters: Winning the Fight Against Imperialism.* New York: Penguin Books, 2004.

Young, Pamela Dickey. "Beyond Moral Influence to an Atoning Life." *Theology Today* Vol. 52 Issue 3 (October 1995): 344-355.

Also from Energion Publications

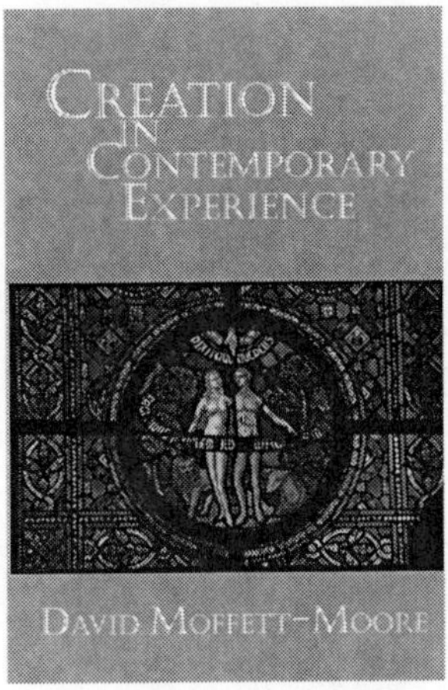

Readers of this book will gain new insights into the mystery of the Creator of Creation.

Herold Weiss
Professor emeritus of New Testament
St. Mary's College, Notre Dame-
Author of *Creation in Scripture*

This text is profound without being preachy, and inspires the reader to claim a faith that is adventurous and world-changing.

Bruce Epperly
Author of *Process Theology: Embracing Adventure with God*

Can liberal and conservative Christianity find a place of meeting?

More from Energion Publications

CPSIA information can be obtained
at www.ICGtesting.com
Printed in the USA
FFOW04n0637180817
38877FF

9 781631 993985